Big Messy Art

Additional Gryphon House books by Mary Ann F. Kohl

Preschool Art

Making Make-Believe

Cooking Art with Jean Potter

Global Art with Jean Potter

MathArts with Cindy Gainer

Bright Ring Publishing books by MaryAnn F. Kohl

Mudworks

Scribble Art

Discovering Great Artists with Kim Solga

Good Earth Art with Cindy Gainer

ScienceArts with Jean Potter

Gryphon House books are available at special discount when purchased in bulk for special premiums and sales promotions as well as for fund-raising use. Special editions or book excerpts also can be created to specification. For details, contact the Director of Marketing at the address below.

10726 Tucker Street, Beltsville, MD 20705

Certificate of Admiration

recognizing

_____

for having
Adventurous Spirit, Youthful Energy,
and Commitment to Children's Creativity

by providing art experiences from

The Big Messy Art Book

by MaryAnn F. Kohl

signed by the author

MaryAnn Kohl

Published by Gryphon House®, Inc.   800.638.0928   www.gryphonhouse.com

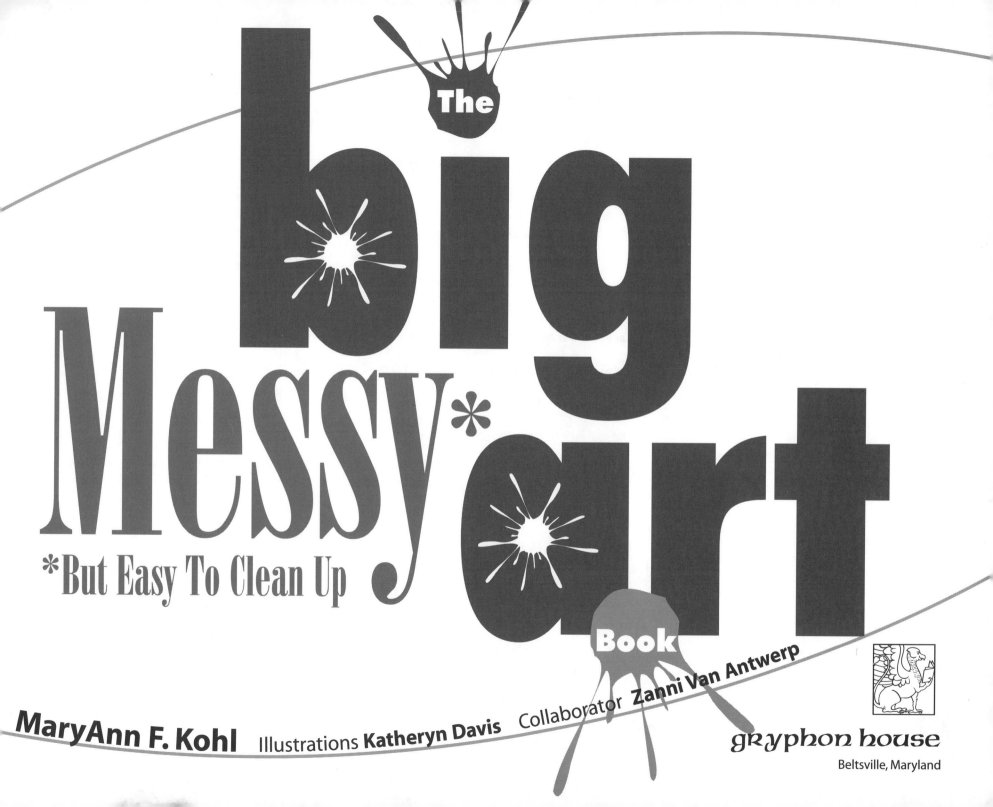

The big Messy* art

Messy

*But Easy To Clean Up

Book

MaryAnn F. Kohl   Illustrations **Katheryn Davis**   Collaborator **Zanni Van Antwerp**

gryphon house

Beltsville, Maryland

for Michael
–MaryAnn

To my son, Sam–we're the two musketeers
–Katheryn

Special Thanks and Recognition to Collaborator, Zanni Van Antwerp

Zanni Van Antwerp met author, MaryAnn Kohl, through an Internet teacher's sharing group where they exchanged ideas and support for several years. Zanni agreed to collaborate with MaryAnn on developing the ideas in The Big Messy Art Book by contributing her marvelous hands-on experiences and writings, working closely with MaryAnn towards the culmination of this adventurous art book. MaryAnn says, "Without Zanni, this book would not be nearly so much fun or quite so wonderful! Zanni adds a special touch. Thanks, Zanni!"

Zanni has been in the early childhood field for more than 20 years and is currently owner and director of Child's Play Preschool, a parent participation school in Palmdale, California. Zanni likes to think of herself more as a facilitator than a teacher. She says, "If there was ever a subject near and dear to my heart, it is art that is big and messy! I'm happy to share my ideas. Thanks, MaryAnn!"
Zanni and her husband Jim live in Palmdale with their three children: Chris 14, Caitlin 12, and Mary 8.

Copyright © 2000 MaryAnn F. Kohl
Published by Gryphon House, Inc.
10726 Tucker Street, Beltsville, MD 20705

World Wide Web: http://www.gryphonhouse.com

Library of Congress Cataloging-in-Publication Data

Kohl, Mary Ann F.
   The big messy art book : but easy to clean up / Mary Ann F. Kohl.
      p. cm.
   Includes bibliogaphical references and index.
   ISBN 0-87659-206-X
   1. Art--Technique--Handbooks, manuals, etc. 2. Artists' materials--Handbooks, manuals, etc. I. Title.

N7430 .K595 2000
372.5'2044--dc2l   00-024515

Table of Contents

Table of Contents

Pat Yourself on the Back

Congratulations on selecting *The Big Messy Art Book*! You have proven yourself to be someone who cares about creativity, and you are to be applauded for your energetic and creative spirit and your willingness to provide artists with a wealth of exciting art experiences.

The Big Messy Art Book is a compilation of art experiences that may take a bit more time to set up, might make a splatter or two on the floor and leave a sticky bucket to rinse out, but the creative process and artistic experiences far outweigh the extra effort. Wait until you see artists dive into new big, messy experiences with enthusiasm and energy. Cleaning up can also be part of the creative process, and the fun!

Many artists have never explored the grander scale of art and all its possibilities. They are ready for the challenge; all they need is the opportunity. The exciting projects in this book take them beyond the ordinary and into the amazing! When they gaze at a skyscraper and ponder its size and structure, you will have given them the breadth of creative experience to imagine how it came to be. When they stroll through an art gallery and look at huge paintings or sculptures, you will have given them the depth of artistic experiences to appreciate what they see. *The Big Messy Art Book* will open the door for artists to experience art on a grander—and yes, often messier—scale with their entire bodies and minds deeply involved in the learning. Add a little splatter, a little moosh, a little splot into art, and thrills, wonder, and amazement are just around the corner!

Display your Certificate of Admiration with pride.

Certificate of Admiration

Recognizing

_____

for having
Adventurous Spirit, Youthful Energy,
and Commitment to Children's Creativity
by providing art experiences from

The Big Messy Art Book

by MaryAnn F. Kohl

by the author   *MaryAnn Kohl*   signed

Published by Gryphon House®, Inc.   800.638.0928   www.gryphonhouse.com

Big Messy Tips

Art clothes and art shoes—instead of wearing a
paint apron or old shirt, artists should wear old play clothes and old
shoes that are okay to get paint, dye, glue, or other messy materials on
that may not wash out. This will enable the artists to be as creative as
they wish, instead of worrying about drips and splats on their best jeans
and expensive shoes. Wear art clothes often. They become more unique
over time.

Bucket of warm soapy water and old
towels—with most of the projects in this book, it's a good idea to
put out sponges, warm soapy water, and old towels so artists can clean
hands, tidy up, or clean up splatters as needed.

Indoor and outdoor space—most activities can be
done indoors or outdoors. Activities that are likely to be more successful
if set up outdoors are noted. However, with many activities, the outdoors
will enable the artist to be more free to express his or her
creativity.

Newspaper-covered workspace—if working
inside (and outside for some
activities), cover the workspace,
whether it is a table, the floor, a
chair, or a countertop. It's a lot
easier to roll up many sheets of
newspaper and find a clean
space underneath, than to clean
up an uncovered workspace.

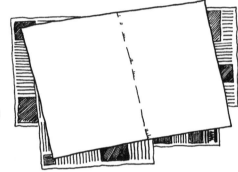

Shallow containers—are often mentioned in
"Materials." Shallow contain-
ers that the author has used
include cookie sheets, flat
baking pans, clean kitty-lit-
ter trays, plastic cafeteria
trays, and painters' pans.

Wet sponge for wiping fingers—is a simple
version of a bucket of warm soapy water and old towels (see note on
this page).

Work space—if the project is set up indoors, protect walls,
floors (maybe ceilings!), and any furniture that might be damaged by
paint or any art material.

The Author's Favorite Materials

BioColor paints—are known for their brilliance and versatility.

Butcher paper or craft paper—is heavy paper that comes on wide rolls in many colors and is available at art or school supply stores. It is often measured in yards, then cut according to need. Better yet, buy your own big roll from an art supply catalog to use for years to come! Free paper source suggestions: Your local newspaper printer may be willing to save the roll ends of newsprint for you. Roll ends, about twelve feet (4 m) wide, are cardboard tubes with wide newsprint rolled on them and can be sawed in half to make two large six-foot (2 m) rolls, or sawed into three or four smaller rolls. (The cardboard tubes inside the rolls come in handy too!)

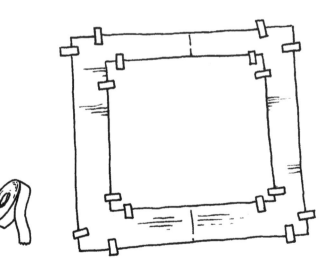

Drywall mud—is a putty-like plaster available in buckets or tubs from hardware and building supply stores.

Hot-Glue Gun—offers instant, long-lasting adhesion, but is recommended only with adult control and supervision.

Liquid Watercolor paints—are great for any project because of their unique properties, such as brightness and transparency. They come in clear colors and in metallic colors.

Ross Art Paste—is perfect for papier-mâché and comes as dried powder in a package. Each package is added to one gallon (4 L) of water. The paste can be pre-made, it holds well, and it dries clear. It is a perfect alternative to wallpaper paste from the hardware store. Mix up in a one-gallon tub with a lid, which then doubles as a great storage container.

Using the Icons

Experience Level

Use the experience icon to choose a project based on how easy or difficult it might be for the artist. Each chapter begins with the simplest activities and ends with the most complicated.

One star for beginning artists with little art experience

Two stars for artists with some art experience

Three stars for artists with more experience

Caution

The caution icon indicates activities that use sharp utensils, a heat source, or any other potentially dangerous materials.

Preparation and Planning

Use the Preparation and Planning icon to gauge how easy or difficult it is for the adult to prepare and set up the activity.

① easy to find materials, easy quick set-up

② familiar materials, moderate set-up

③ unusual materials, involved set-up

Messy Meter

Prepare the art area for the level of messiness with this helpful messiness level indicator.

A little bit messy

Somewhat messy

Very messy

Chapter 1
Action Art

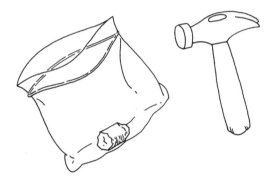

Sidewalk Paint

What a smashing idea! Crushing and grinding sidewalk chalk is an inexpensive way to make your own sidewalk paint for small or large murals! This big messy idea washes away with a hose or the next rain.

MATERIALS

large sidewalk chalk
heavy zipper-closure plastic bags
hammers, mallets, or blocks
containers
water
paintbrushes

PROCESS

1. Break the sidewalk chalk into five to fifteen pieces.
2. Put a big piece of sidewalk chalk into a heavy zipper-closure plastic bag and close.
3. Carefully pound chalk into a powder with a hammer or block.
Hint: Use care when hammering; supervise closely.
4. Put the chalk powder into a container. Add water and stir with a paintbrush until it is the consistency of paint. Make several colors.
5. Paint on the sidewalk with the new paint. Or, pour big puddles of paint on the sidewalk and drive through them with large toy trucks, trikes, or bikes.
6. Wash the paint away with a hose and water, or let the rain wash it away over time.

VARIATIONS

Mix powdered colors together in a plastic bag to make new colors, then add water.
Grind chalk and put into little bowls. Dip a wet paintbrush in the chalk and paint with it on paper.
Place butcher paper on the sidewalk. Drive trikes or bikes through paint and then onto the paper.
Walk through the paint puddles with shoes or barefoot to make footprints.
Paint on walls, fences, or steps (with permission, of course!).
Use a mortar and pestle to make a finer powder.

Foot Sponge Painting

Sponge painting—with a new twist that's bound to cause tons of laughter and great big art all at once. Strap big sponges on your feet, step in the paint, and go paint walkin'.

PROCESS

1. Place long sheets of butcher paper on the floor. Tape down for safety.
2. Put tempera paint in two shallow pans, one color for each pan. Make more pans of paint if you want more than two colors. Place next to the paper.
3. Take off shoes and socks. Strap a sponge to each foot with Velcro straps. With adult help, step in two pans of paint—one color for each foot.

Hint: This is a slippery activity; one or two adults should support the artist.

4. With adult assistance, walk across the paper, creating sponge designs.
5. After removing straps, rinse bare feet in a tub of warm, soapy water. Use old towels to dry. More soap and scrubbing may be needed in the shower or bathtub.

MATERIALS

big butcher paper
masking tape
tempera paint
sturdy, shallow pans
big sponges
Velcro straps (from sporting, bike, and hardware stores)
plastic dish tub of warm soapy water
old towels

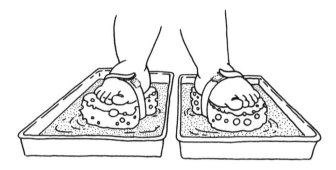

VARIATIONS

Start with only one foot strapped with a sponge before trying both.

Cut sponges into shapes.

Tape three or four sheets of paper together creating a "skating rink" and skate on some pastel blue paint, with adult help.

Spray the paper with water and step into powdered tempera paint.

Instead of sponges, try dust mops or scrub brushes attached to feet.

Make sock paintings, feet paintings, boot paintings, and so on.

Spinning Painting

Swirling jewelry chains dipped in paint create beautiful, unique circles of overlapping colors. Bright, fluorescent paint makes this a gorgeous visual experience.

MATERIALS

8"-18" (20 cm-50 cm) lengths of jewelry chain

tempera paint

big sheets of paper

TEMPERA PAINT

PROCESS

1. Garage sales are good places to find old jewelry. Strings of beads work great for this activity too.

Hint: Jewelry chains are perfect for gentle spinning, but experiment with other types of chain, such as beaded chain, strings of beads, clothesline rope, or twine and string.

2. Practice spinning the chain. To do this, hold onto the end link or fastener. Hold the chain against some paper on the table. Make the chain spin in a flat, circular motion, round and round. Keep the pincher and thumb close to the paper.

3. Now for the real thing! Dip a chain in any color of paint. It's not necessary to dip fingers into the paint. Keep about 1"-2" (3 cm-5 cm) of chain paint-free. Hold this part of the chain during the dipping process.

4. Let the chain drip for a moment over the paint.

5. Now gently spin the painted chain (remember step 2?) right on the paper. Spin until no more paint comes off of the chain.

6. Dip the chain in another color and spin again! It's pretty to let colors overlap each other on the paper.

7. Rinse chains clean in clear water when done.

VARIATIONS

Twirl a string that is weighted with a button or washer tied on the end.

Tape paper to a wall and dangle painted chains on it. Swing them over the paper. (Put paper on the floor to catch any drips.)

BIG MESSY ART

Tennis Toss

Stand back from the wall, wind up, and hurl the tennis ball at the wall.
What's so special about throwing a ball? Dip it in paint first!

PROCESS

1. Tape big paper or cardboard to a wall outdoors. Be sure this is a wall on which you don't mind getting paint; otherwise, protect the wall as needed.
2. Fill shallow pans with tempera paint and place them on the ground at a safe throwing distance from the wall. Place the dishpan of tennis balls nearby too.
3. Put on work gloves, if you like.
4. Roll a tennis ball in paint. Wind up and throw the ball at the paper. Whap! It will make a fuzzy, splattery print.

Clean-up tip: Now the ball is also rolling across the ground or bumping into people's feet, so be prepared for extra paint here and there. You might like to set up a cardboard appliance box that has been cut open as a "holding chamber" for the ball toss. Tape the paper on the opened box, with the edges folded in.

5. Use the same ball or a different one, and throw some more prints at the paper. Work until the paper is filled with prints.
6. Rinse the balls in clear water under a hose, squeeze dry with an old towel, and let dry in the dishpan until another day.

MATERIALS

outdoor wall or fence
tape
big paper or card-
   board
tempera paint
shallow pans
old tennis balls (still
   fuzzy!)
dishpan for holding
   tennis balls
work gloves, optional
hose and old towels

VARIATIONS

Hold the ball, dip in paint, and rub paint on paper.
With a gentle underhand lop, toss the painty ball onto paper on the ground.
Drop a paint-filled ball from a height and let it bounce on paper on the ground.

Snap Painting

Picture this snappy idea—*a picture frame, some rubber bands, and paint. Stretch rubber bands across the frame, then coat with paint. Snap the rubber bands over a piece of paper to create a snappy masterpiece!*

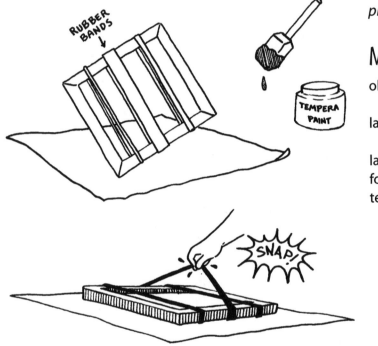

Materials

old sturdy picture
  frame
large, strong rubber
  bands
large pieces of paper
foam paintbrushes
tempera paint in
  containers

Process

1. Stretch several rubber bands over the empty frame. Use one rubber band or many.
2. Place a sheet of paper on the table, then set the frame over the paper.
3. Paint rubber bands carefully and completely with foam brushes dipped in paint. Mixing colors is fine.
4. Grab a rubber band, stretch it upward, and then let go. Snap! It snaps against the paper making a splattering design.
5. Snap any other rubber bands that still have paint on them.
6. Add more paint as necessary.
7. Remove the paper, and start over with a new snap design. The rubber bands may need to be wiped clean with a wet sponge. It's up to the artist. Some like leftover paint to remain on the bands for special effects of mixing colors.

Clean-up tip: Hands are becoming very painty by now, so keep a bucket of soapy water and old towels handy. Another suggestion is a large wet sponge right on the table for wiping fingers.

Variations

Use a big frame with one color only, moving and turning the frame to achieve different designs on the paper.

Use smaller frames, each with a different color, moving them around the paper.

Use light or neon paint on black paper.

Use sewing elastic in place of rubber bands.

Slap Painting

Fill a sock with sand, tie a knot, dip it in some paint, and slap a painting on the paper!

PROCESS

1. Put sand in the sock (or the cut-off foot of old panty hose) until it's about the size of a fist. Tie a knot in the sock close to the sand. Make it tight! Make a sandy sock for each color of paint.
2. Tape paper to the newspaper-covered work area.
3. Pour paint into pans or bowls about 1" (3 cm) deep.
4. Dip a sandy sock into the paint and then *slap* the sock on the paper.
5. Slap with as many different colors as needed to satisfy the design.
6. Make more paintings!

MATERIALS

old trouser socks or panty hose
sand
tape
paper
work area covered with newspaper
tempera paint
bowls or pie pans
butcher paper

VARIATIONS

Drop the sandy paint sock from a high place onto the paper.

Fill socks with pea gravel, aquarium rocks, or marbles. Heavier socks should be slapped against paper that is on the ground, instead of on a table.

Experiment with different types of socks.

Dip sandy socks in water, then in powdered tempera paint, then slap on the paper.

Dip dry sandy socks in powdered tempera paint and slap on wet paper.

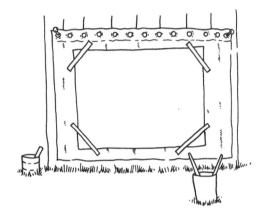

Splatter Paint

Big and messy is the name of the game! Be brave! Get some big brushes
and some paint, and "throw" a paint party!

MATERIALS

paint containers
tempera paint
plastic sheet or tarp
tape
butcher paper
big paintbrushes

PROCESS

1. Fill the containers with different colors of paint.
2. Protect the wall with plastic sheeting or a tarp. Old shower curtains work great! Then tape the paper to the plastic. (Working
   outside minimizes cleanup.)
3. Now for the fun: Dip a brush in paint, then *fling* the paint onto the
   paper, just like the famous artist Jackson Pollock.
4. Add more colors.
5. Experiment with gentle flings and hearty flings to see the results.
6. Dry the painting on the wall, or remove and make another.

VARIATIONS

Fling water onto the paper and then sprinkle powdered tempera
   paint onto the drops.
Take the painting off the wall, place on the floor, and sprinkle some
   glitter into the wet paint.
Work on a tarp on the floor instead of the wall.
Work on paper taped to a fence outdoors.
Explore the work of Jackson Pollock and imitate his style by paint-
   ing with some of the following techniques:

dab	drizzle	smear	sprinkle
dabble	fleck	smudge	streak
dapple	fling	spatter	striate
daub	plop	speckle	swab
dot	plunk	splatter	throw
drip	shake	spray	trickle

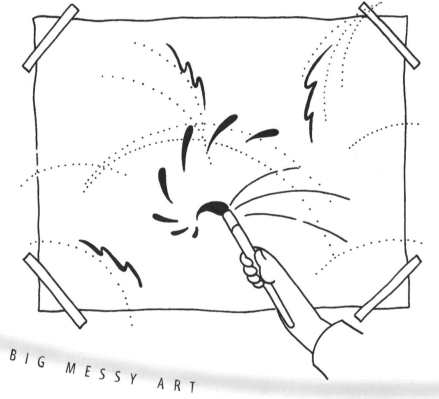

Race Painting

It doesn't matter if you win or lose; it's how awesome the paper looks when the race ends! See the paint drops rolling downhill, speeding and mixing with the science of gravity.

PROCESS

1. Cut the plywood or cardboard about 3'-5' (1 m-2 m) long and 15" (40 cm) wide, or as wide as a baking pan.
2. Spread newspapers on the floor.
3. Place the baking pan on top of the newspapers.
4. Lean one end of the board on a table or chair and place the other end in the shallow baking pan.
5. Secure the board with some tape or string.
6. Tape a piece of butcher paper to the board, covering the full length of the board.
7. Mix about three parts water to one part paint in containers. Put one color of paint in each container.
8. With eyedroppers or pipettes, drip paint toward the top edge of the paper and watch it race to the bottom. Keep adding drops and see how they mix and make tracks. The drips will fall into the shallow baking dish.
9. Remove the paper when satisfied with the design, then tape on a new sheet and start all over again.

VARIATIONS

Try a race: Ready! Set! Two to four people each drop a different color at the top edge of the paper, all at the same time. Go! Off the drops go, racing down the paper.

Use only primary color paint to make secondary colors.

Use complimentary colors (red, yellow, and orange for example) and paint with the drips that collect in the pan.

MATERIALS

plywood, particle board, or very sturdy cardboard
saw or sharp scissors (adult only)
shallow baking pan
newspapers
table or chair
tape or string
butcher paper
watercolor paint or any thin paint
small containers
eyedroppers or pipettes

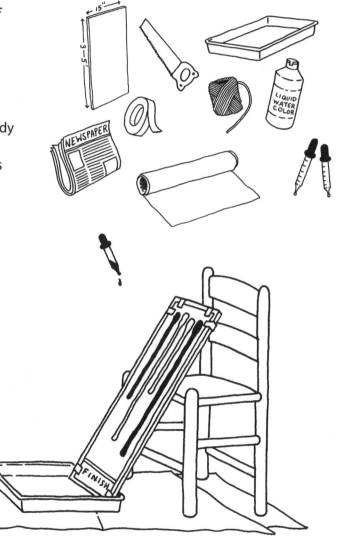

Bubble Painting

Explore an airy world of powdery paint that is sifted over paper. Then pop kaleidoscopic bubbles forming circles of design.

MATERIALS

big sheets of paper
tape
old flour sifter
spoons
powdered tempera
   paint
homemade bubble
   solution recipe (see
   below) or commer-
   cial bubble solution
bubble wands or bub-
   ble tools (see list)

HOMEMADE BUBBLE SOLUTION RECIPE

2 cups (500 mL) dishwashing detergent (Dawn works very well)
6 cups (1.5 L) water
3/4 cup (175 mL) light corn syrup
1 gallon (4 L) container with a tight-fitting lid
Mix the above ingredients in a container with a lid. Shake and let
   settle for four hours. This recipe can be halved or doubled.

BUBBLE WANDS OR BUBBLE TOOLS TO TRY

clean funnel
coat hanger (any kind)
empty thread spools
heavy wire shapes
kitchen whisk
plastic berry basket
potato masher
six pack plastic rings
slotted spoon
toy bubble wands
wide sieve colander
your hand (OK sign)

YOUR OWN HAND!

POP!

POP!

POP!

Bubble Painting (continued)

Process

1. Spread the big sheets of paper on the floor. Tape sheets together to form extra big pieces. Work indoors or out.
2. Set an old flour sifter on the paper. Spoon no more than 3-4 tablespoons (45 mL-60 mL) of dry tempera into the sifter. Use one color, or mix several colors together.
3. Sift the powdered paint over the paper wherever you wish.
4. Change the powdered paint to bubble designs by blowing bubbles with wands or tools (see list of suggestions on previous page). Let the bubbles drift down on the painting and pop in the sifted, powdery paint. POP! A bright design appears!

Hint: Some tools will give billowy bubbles, others small individual bubbles, and others large wet bubbles. Each will produce a different design.

5. Blow bubbles and make bubble paint designs all over the paper.
6. Add more paint and bubbles to make an even bigger design!

Variations

Spray water lightly from bottles on sifted, powdered tempera paint.
Spray watercolor paint (or food coloring mixed with water) from bottles onto powdered tempera paint.

Hair Dryer Painting

Ping-Pong balls covered in paint are blown around paper with a hair dryer, creating hair-raising designs!

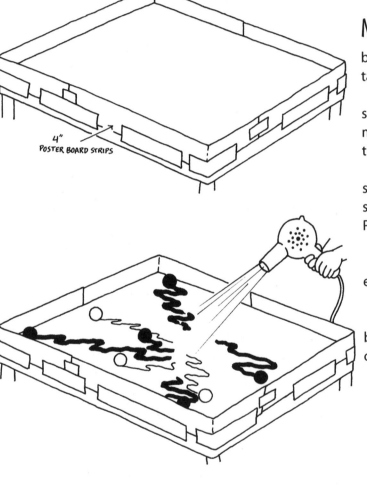

4"
POSTER BOARD STRIPS

MATERIALS

butcher paper
tag board or poster
    board
scissors
masking tape
thin tempera or water-
    color paint
small cups or bowls
spoons
Ping-Pong balls or
    other lightweight
    balls
electric hair dryer
    (with adult supervi-
    sion)
bowl of clear water
old towels

PROCESS

1. Cover table with butcher paper.
2. Cut tag board or poster board into strips 4" (10 cm) wide.
3. Tape the 4" (10 cm) poster board strips around the edge of the table, making a continuous border that will keep the balls from rolling off the table.
4. Put about 1 1/2" (4 cm) of paint in each cup or bowl. Place one spoon in each color.
5. Plop a Ping-Pong ball in each cup. Roll it over in the paint in the cup to coat.
6. Use a spoon to pick up a ball and drop it on the paper. Use one color and ball, or add several colors and balls.
7. Blow the painted balls around the table with the blow dryer.
Hint: As always, use CAUTION with electrical cords and electricity. Adult supervision required. Keep water away from the hair dryer.
8. Rinse Ping-Pong balls in a big bowl of clear water, and dry with an old towel before reusing.

VARIATIONS

Make small puddles of thin paint on the paper; blow the Ping-Pong balls through the puddles creating lines of design.
Use your own blow power (pucker and blow) to roll the balls about.

Punctured Balloon

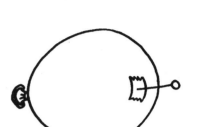

Imagine squirting a controlled tiny, steady stream of paint from a *punctured balloon directly onto a sheet of paper!*

PROCESS

1. Place large sheets of paper on the ground before beginning.
2. With adult help, squirt a generous amount of paint directly into the balloon. Several tablespoons will do. Then finish filling the balloon with water. Tie the balloon to close. Swirl a little to mix the water and paint.
3. Make several balloons with different colors of paint inside.
4. Carefully poke a pinhole in the balloon. If this is difficult, put a piece of tape on the balloon before puncturing it. Repeat for other balloons.
5. Now for the fun! Aim streams of paint at the paper directly from the balloons. Create designs, mixing colors as desired.
6. Allow the painting to dry where it is.

VARIATIONS

Puncture the balloon with more than one hole. Work quickly!
Squirt paint from a high place, like a chair, ladder, or tabletop.
Tape the paper to a wall, cover the drip area on the floor, and squirt paint on the wall.
Smear the paint squirt designs with a spatula or a rectangle of cardboard, mixing colors and designs together on the paper.

MATERIALS

butcher paper
balloons
Liquid Watercolors or thinned tempera paint
water
needle or pin
tape, optional

Wading Pool Ball Painting

Painting with balls in a wading pool becomes an activity with grand results! The artists rock, roll, and spin the painted balls to create BIG paintings with unusual patterns.

MATERIALS

tempera paint
containers, such as
    plastic pitchers
balls of all sizes (see
    list)
large sheets of paper
small wading pool,
    solid plastic type
4 or more artists
spoons or tongs

BALLS TO TRY

baby's ball
cat ball
dog ball
golf ball
Nerf ball
rubber ball
small playground ball
softball
tennis ball
whiffle ball

PROCESS

1. Place two or three balls in containers, each filled with about a cup (250 mL) of paint. Plastic pitchers with handles work great, leaving one hand free.
2. Place a large sheet of paper in the bottom of the wading pool.
3. Four or more artists pick up the pool by the edges and lift it a few inches off the ground.
4. One artist uses a spoon or tongs to lift the balls out of the paint, and then plop them in the pool on the large paper.
5. The artists tip and move the pool around cooperatively, rolling the paint balls around the paper, making designs.
6. Remove the paper when done, and dry.
7. Make more paintings, experimenting with different ball sizes.

VARIATIONS

Artists can take turns as the "painted-ball supplier," dropping the balls into the paint and placing them into the pool.
Experiment with different types and sizes of balls. For example, golf balls make little dots and tennis balls make fuzzy designs.
Collect several different types of dog toy balls with interesting textures for painting.

Water Balloon Splat

Simply fill up balloons *with paint and water and then let them fly! For the most adventurous artists only!*

PROCESS

1. Protect the art area or outdoor area with plastic on the floor or ground as needed.
2. Tape together two pieces of 6' (2 m) craft or butcher paper edge to edge to form one big square that is 6' x 6' (2 m x 2 m). Tape this large sheet to the plastic or use bricks or rocks as weights on the ground.
3. Stand the chair or short ladder to the side of the paper.
4. With adult help, prepare the balloons. Squirt a generous amount of paint into a balloon from the spout on the bottle, then fill the rest of the way with water. Tie the balloon closed, so the balloon is tight and ready to break.

Hint: Stick a funnel into the end of the balloon. Pour the paint into the balloon and then fill with water to finish. Remove the funnel and tie the balloon closed.

5. Fill many balloons with different colors. Keep them in a plastic tub until the project begins.
6. The artist climbs up on the chair or ladder beside the paper. Someone hands the artist a paint-filled balloon, which is then dropped onto the paper to splatter and make a big design. Splat! Add more dropped balloons in different colors.
7. Make several balloon splat paintings.
8. When done, hose the outdoor area clean. If done indoors, fold the plastic sheet and carry it outside to be hosed clean.

MATERIALS

plastic sheet
tape
butcher paper or craft paper
chair or kitchen ladder
small water balloons
Liquid Watercolors or thinned tempera paint
water
plastic tub

Rubber Glove Painting

It's as easy as milking a cow! Just the thought of squirting paint from a rubber glove onto paper is enough to bring a smile to any artist's face, young or old! One thing is for sure: this is a very messy art project, but worth every squirt!

MATERIALS

plastic sheeting
masking tape
several 6' (2 m) long
   sheets of craft paper
several pairs of rubber
   gloves
nail
thinned tempera paint
rubber bands (the
   large hefty kind)
dish pans

PROCESS

1. Tape plastic sheeting on the floor, ground, or table, allowing at least 3' (1m) extra around the edges of the craft paper.
2. Place the craft paper on the plastic. Tape it down too. Working outside is best. Cleaning up is easier, and artists can take off their shoes and enjoy the outdoors! Otherwise, work in a large open space indoors.
4. Next prick holes in the fingertip of each rubber glove with a nail. Experiment with the size of the hole. If the hole is too small it will not work, but a hole too large will only ooze paint. Start small; making the hole bigger is always possible.
Hint: Heavy rubber gloves work best.
4. Thin tempera paint with water. Make plenty of each color and be ready to refill gloves as needed.
Clean-up tip: Add a few drops of liquid soap to each color of paint for easier cleanup.
5. Fill each glove with one color of paint. Fill to the wrist, then tightly secure the arm with a heavy rubber band. Place each glove in a pan, one for each color. The gloves will leak a little so the pan helps with the mess.
6. Ready, set, paint! Gently squeeze the fingers of a glove to see how the paint squirts out on the paper. If the hole isn't big enough, increase its size now. The paint will squirt out like milking a cow. Squeezing the middle of the glove will produce an all-over sprinkler!
7. Refill gloves as needed.

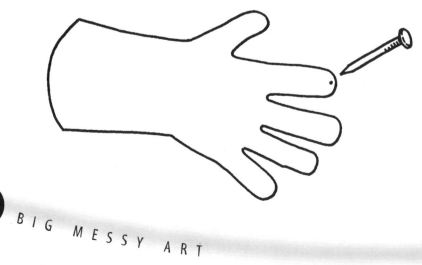

Rubber Glove Painting (continued)

VARIATION

Staple the filled rubber glove to the underside of a bench and create a "milk the cow" activity.

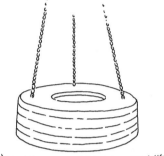

Living Pendulum Art

Find a playground with a tire swing that hangs parallel to the ground from several chains. It will make the perfect pendulum for creating living art!

MATERIALS

tire swing
big sheet of cardboard
big sheets of paper,
   rolled up
tape or rocks
colored markers

PROCESS

1. Locate a playground or park that has a tire swing, the kind that hangs from a tripod of chains and swings parallel to the ground. (See illustration.) Other types of swings will work for creating swing art, but will not give the pendulum effect of swinging in multi-directions.
2. The artist lies on his or her tummy on the tire swing, facing toward the ground.
3. Slip the large sheet of cardboard under the artist on the swing. Then unroll a large sheet of paper on the cardboard. Tape the corners down or weight with rocks.
4. Hand the artist two uncapped, open markers, one for each hand. Now push the tire swing as the artist lets the markers swipe the paper again and again, creating pendulum designs. Change marker colors if the artist requests.
5. Experiment with different directions of swinging to create different designs. Use both sides of the paper, too!
6. Pull the paper and cardboard out from under the swing before the artist jumps down.

VARIATIONS

Paint living pendulum designs instead of using markers.
Try making "swing designs" from traditional forward and backward swings.

Roaster Pan Painting

Cook up a drippy project that takes two to hold the punctured roaster pan, and another to pour in the paint. Rock the pan as it drips onto paper below, creating a splittery-splattery, drippity-droppity work of art in color.

Process

1. With adult help, poke several small holes in the bottom of the roaster pan with a pencil or the points of a pair of scissors. Start with only a few. More holes can be added later once you see how things go.
2. To begin, set the roaster pan on the plastic tray next to a sheet of butcher paper.
3. Pour paint into the roaster, one color or several puddles of different colors. Start with a little; add more later on.
4. Two artists take hold of the pan together, holding it over a big sheet of butcher paper. They rock the pan slowly over the butcher paper, watching the paint drip out and spatter on the paper.
5. A third artist can help change the colors to keep the dripping going full time, or the two can set the pan down on the tray and add more colors on their own!
6. Other paper can be slipped under the dripping pan at any time to make more and more paintings.
7. When finished, rinse the pan and tray in clear water. (Artists often enjoy watching the colored rinse water run down a white sink.)

Variation

Drip paint from a drinking straw. Hold a finger over the top of a straw, place in paint, remove, and release finger so paint drips onto the paper.

Materials

big aluminum roaster pan
pencil or scissors
plastic tray
large sheet of butcher paper
Liquid Watercolors or thinned tempera paint
2 artists to hold the pan
1 artist to pour paint

Spray Dye Towel

Art for the beach or bath! *Hang a towel over the fence. Ready? Aim, then fire that dye to make an inexpensive, colorful towel like no other!*

MATERIALS

1 package dye for each color
2 quarts (2 L) water for each color
1 tablespoon salt (15 mL) for each color
2-quart container (2 L) with lids, one for each color
spray bottles
white bath towels (a motel or hotel may donate old, clean towels)
permanent marker
fence or other suitable work area
big safety pins

PROCESS

1. Mix each package of dye according to the directions. (Rit, the dye used for this activity, uses 2 quarts (2 L) water and 1 tablespoon (15 mL) salt.) Also read the instructions on the package for hints for success and washing instructions.
   Clean-up tip: Remember that this is permanent dye, and it will permanently color any clothing or other fabrics with which it comes in contact, so dress accordingly. Working outside helps minimize any accidental color staining indoors.
2. Pour dye into spray bottles.
3. Use a permanent marker to write names or create designs on towels, if desired.
4. Hang the towels on the fence. Use safety pins to secure the towels in place.
5. Now for the fun part! Spray the towels with dye. Let colors mix and blend directly on the towels.
6. Let the towels dry.
7. Follow the directions on the dye package for washing.
8. Use the towels for the beach, for the bath, for gifts, or any other idea.

VARIATION

Spray dye and design other fabric items, such as dishtowels, fabric napkins, hair ribbons, handkerchiefs, headbands, pillowcases, sheets, table runners, tablecloths, throw rugs, T-shirts, and washcloths.

Chapter 2

Basic But Bigger

Big Motion Crayoning

Draw with the biggest arm movements possible—huge circles, dips, and expansive reaching arches and motions! Add fun to the experience by bundling crayons with a big rubber band to make a "crayon clutch." Make two bundles, one for each hand!

Materials

big piece of paper or
   poster board
tape
crayons
big rubber bands

Process

1. Tape the paper or poster board to the wall, with the bottom edge touching the floor, and the top edge higher than the artist can reach in all directions while on tippy toes.

Hint: To make the paper doublewide for the most expansive reaches, tape the seam of two sheets of large paper together. Tape them from top to bottom to prevent tearing.

2. Bundle a handful of crayons with a big rubber band. Make all the crayon tips even by tapping them on a piece of paper and adjusting the rubber band.

3. Stand in front of the huge piece of paper, and make the biggest arm motions possible, bending knees, going way down, and stretching on tippy toes, way up high. Circles, long reaches, arches, and other big, stretching motions are fun to do.

4. Fill the paper until satisfied that the poster is complete.

Variations

This is the perfect activity to do to music.

Use chalk, markers, or paint and brushes.

To make a grand scale crayon resist, paint over the crayoned design with wide soft brushes filled with bright watercolor paint or thinned tempera paint. For extra fun, spread the paint with a straight edge or spatula.

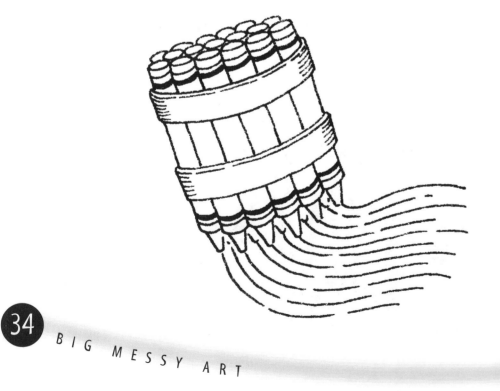

Drip and Fold With a Friend

Artists love to put blobs of paint on a piece of paper, fold it in half, and open it up again to see the magical, blended, symmetric wonder. Here's a way to share the magic with a friend in an all-new activity with exciting, oversized results.

PROCESS

1. Pre-fold paper in half and open up again, placing it on the newspaper-covered floor.
   Hint: Old posters or large sheets of paper from a local print shop's recycle bin work great and come in unusual textures and finishes!
2. Put one color of paint in each cup. Put a spoon in each cup.
3. The artists spoon and drizzle paint onto the paper, or gently squirt paint with a turkey baster on the fold or anywhere on the paper.
4. Working as a team, the two artists help each other fold the paper, pressing gently over the paint and rubbing the folded paper.
5. Unfold the paper and see the wonderful symmetrical design created together.
6. Make another and another, exploring the variations below.

MATERIALS

large sheets of paper
newspaper-covered floor
tempera paint
cups
spoons
turkey baster, optional
2 artists

← PRE-FOLDED

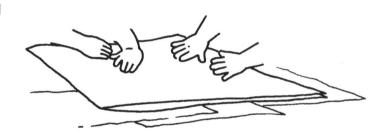

VARIATIONS

Squirt colored glue onto paper instead of paint.
Use paper that has been pre-cut into giant shapes—circles, butterflies, hearts, and so on.
Use colored glue on wax paper or clear plastic for a stained glass look.

Colossal Cube Painting

Get ready for a titanic rendition of ice cube painting! Freeze tempera paint in big bowls and pans with "handles" for several artists to work together. They guide the icy paint chunk around the paper, cooperatively creating a painting together.

MATERIALS

large containers—big
   pots, bowls, pans,
   etc.
water
tempera or watercolor
   paint
foil or plastic wrap
plastic spoons, tongue
   depressors, or popsi-
   cle sticks
freezer
butcher paper
masking tape
warm water
2 or more artists

PROCESS

1. Fill containers with paint and water mixed together.
2. Tightly cover containers with foil or plastic wrap. Make small slits in the cover and place a few spoons or sticks through the slits. The cover holds the stick "handles" in place until the water freezes.
3. Freeze the paint and water overnight or until very solid.
4. Meanwhile, cover a table with butcher paper. Tape the corners with masking tape to hold the paper steady.
5. Dip the containers in warm water to release the colossal paint cubes. Slip the colossal paint cubes onto the paper.
6. Two or more artists move the colossal paint cubes around the paper together, cooperatively holding the handles. The cubes will make paint designs on the paper.

Clean-up tip: Have old towels handy for sopping up dripping paint.

VARIATIONS

Vary the size of the cubes from small (for two artists) to extra large (dishpan size and six handles).

Explore freezing only primary colors. Watch the colors mix on the paper as new colors appear.

Wear mittens or gloves and skip the handles. Messy and fun!

Lawn Prints

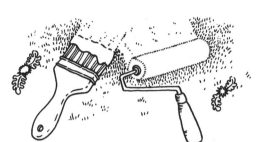

Bring the great outdoors inside to enjoy year round when you paint the lawn with paint rollers and then lift grass prints onto colorful paper.

PROCESS

1. With adult permission, choose a section of the lawn that can be painted.
2. Pour paint into flat pans or containers.
3. Paint the chosen section of lawn with big brushes dipped in paint or paint rollers rolled through paint.
4. Before the paint can dry, place a sheet of paper over the painted area, pat and rub gently, and lift a print of the lawn.
5. Make as many as you wish.
Hint: Craft paper that comes on rolls in school supply and art stores works well; large sheets of construction paper or the backs of used posters also work well.
6. Enjoy the prints as is, or use them as paper for other art projects.
7. Hose the paint from the grass with water when done.

VARIATIONS

Paint and lift prints of other outdoor areas like trees, sidewalks, walls, and playground equipment or other areas that can be easily washed clean with water.

Make prints of painted "patio grass" (Astroturf) or carpet samples.

Cut the dry prints into strips to use for weaving or other art projects. (See pages 88, 95, and 114.)

Paint with clear water (and no paint!) for the fun of seeing wet designs that dry quickly. Rocks look especially shiny!

MATERIALS

large grassy lawn area
tempera paint
shallow containers
big paintbrushes or
   paint rollers
large sheets of paper
hose and water

Doormat Print

Big prints made from doormats have surprising and amazing designs. Paint decorative doormats with large paintbrushes, then lift magnificent doormat prints.

MATERIALS

tempera paint
shallow containers for
    paint
small paint rollers or
    large brushes
doormats with raised,
    textured designs
large sheets of paper
hose and water

PROCESS

1. Fill each container with one color of tempera paint mixed to a smooth, spreadable consistency.
2. Roll a paint roller through some paint. Then roll paint over the entire clean doormat. Use one color, or many colors. Wide paintbrushes work great if rollers are not available.
Hint: Discarded or old mats from garage sales work well. First give them a good vacuuming, shaking, or hose-down to remove dust and debris. Dry if necessary.
3. Spread a sheet of paper over the painted mat. Rub back and forth over the back of the paper with both hands to pick up a print.
4. Peel off the paper, and see the surprising and magnificent print found on the paper.
5. To make another print, you can hose off the paint and start new, but you don't have to. Simply add more paint to the already paint-filled mat and make more prints!
6. When done, wash the paint from the mat with a hose outdoors. Dry the mat and store until the next printing session. Or relegate the clean doormat to a doorway where it can be put to use.

VARIATIONS

Collect a variety of mats, both with designs and with words. Combine a print from one mat with that from a second mat, all on the same sheet of paper.
Place paper on the mat in one direction to make a print. Then repaint the mat, and place paper on it again in a different direction, rotating it 90 degrees

Pelon Design

Make a big beautiful wall hanging from pelon, a fabric used in clothing construction. Fold up a BIG square with a friend, drip on some bright colors, unfold, and voila—a wall hanging that will delight and astonish!

PROCESS

1. With a friend, fold the pelon sheet three or four times in any fashion, much like folding a towel or a piece of paper.
   Hint: Pelon is a fabric backing used for clothing construction and sewing, especially in collars or areas that need stiffening, and is available at all fabric stores. It has somewhat the look and feel of thick coffee filters.
2. Place thick sheets of newspaper or other protective materials over the work area. Then lay the folded pelon on the work area.
3. Put a bit of one color of paint in each cup.
4. Drip paint from spoons onto the pelon, letting it soak and blend in.
5. Artists help each other unfold the pelon and lay it flat on the newspapers. Look at the beautiful symmetrical design.
6. Let it dry for several hours until completely dry. Hang in a window with push pins to enjoy the light shining through the colors.
7. Optional display ideas for a wall hanging:
     stretch and staple the pelon to a wooden frame
     stretch the pelon over a piece of cardboard, wrapping the edges around to the back and taping

MATERIALS

2 or more artists
large square pieces of pelon
newspaper, an old shower curtain, or a tarp
Liquid Watercolors or liquid fabric dyes
cups and spoons
push pins

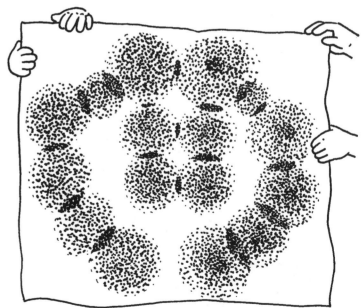

VARIATIONS

Cut the pelon into smaller squares and create flower blossoms. Gather the pelon in the center and wrap with a piece of wire, which is also the stem. Display the bouquet in a vase or container.

Texture Board

Make beautiful gallery-sized prints, each a unique masterpiece! The texture board is basically adult-made, but the creativity belongs to the artist.

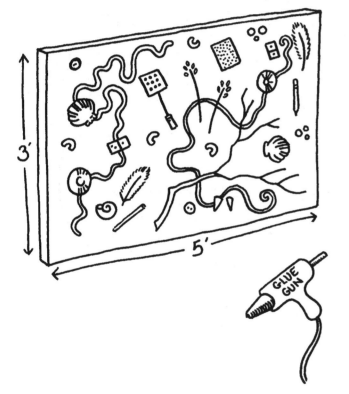

MATERIALS

plywood board, about 3' x 5' (1 m x 1 1/2 m)
materials for the textures (see list)
contact cement and brush, or hot glue gun (adult only)

MAKING THE TEXTURE BOARD (ADULT)

ADULT PROCESS WITH ARTIST INPUT

1. Glue texture pieces on the plywood board, covering the entire board in any design. The artist assists with the design, but an adult uses the contact cement or hot glue gun to construct the board.
   Hint: Put contact cement on both the board and the texture pieces, so they will adhere to each other.
2. Let dry completely before making prints. Keep the following in mind:
   Make sure the area is well ventilated.
   Keep the height of the textured pieces fairly uniform and level for better printing results.
   Use thin plastic or wood scraps to build up thinner items (tile, for example).

TEXTURED MATERIALS TO TRY

bingo markers	scraps of plastic buttons
buttons	small branches
ceramic tiles	tie spacers
old license plates	tree bark
parts of old toys	anything with interesting
pebbles	texture
poker chips	

Texture Board (continued)

Making Texture Board Prints (artist)

Materials

texture board
brushes and/or paint rollers
tempera paint
butcher paper or large sheets of paper

Process

1. Paint over the texture board with several colors of paint, covering the entire board or simply selecting a section of the board for the print.
2. Place the paper on the painted board and rub the back of the paper.
3. Lift a print.
4. Set aside to dry.
5. Make more prints, experimenting with where colors are placed.

Variations

Add a little glue to the paint and sprinkle the finished print with glitter.
Use holiday colors to create unique printed wrapping paper.
Large prints make beautiful backgrounds for photo collages or artwork.
Printed paper can be cut into strips for weaving or other art projects.

Giant Stamps

Stamps and inkpads are very popular. *All that's needed for this project is a good case of stamp fever to create huge stamps.*

Materials

plywood or particle-
board
thin sheets of dense
foam, like that from
wetsuits or comput-
er mouse pads
scissors
hot glue gun (adult
only)
empty thread spools
old hand towels
shallow containers
tempera paint
big sheets of paper

Process

1. When acquiring the wood, have it cut it into squares about 6"
   (15cm) wide.
   Hint: Discounted sheets of board are often available at hardware or
   building stores.
2. Cut foam into designs and shapes like circles, squares, teardrops,
   letters, flowers, animals, etc. An adult can glue the shapes to the
   board with a hot glue gun. The artist directs the design.
3. An adult hot glues a spool to the middle of the other side of the
   board for a pressing handle.
4. To make the pad, fold an old hand towel into fourths. Place in a
   shallow container and soak with paint. Make one pad for each
   color of paint.
5. Press the Giant Stamp onto the paint pad and then onto paper,
   making giant designs.

Variations

For a Stamp Block, hot glue (adult only) foam shapes on all six sides
   of a cube of wood. Roll the cube on a paint pad, and then roll
   onto the paper.
Experiment creating very large or very small stamps.

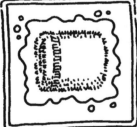

FOLD AN OLD HAND TOWEL
INTO FOURTHS.....
SOAK WITH PAINT
TO MAKE A PAD.

Titanic Simple Weave

Save a big piece of *heavy cardboard for constructing a weaving that requires no expertise, only determination and all the yarn you can find!*

PROCESS

1. With adult help, cut a piece of cardboard into a 3' x 3' (1 m x 1 m) size or any other size the artist desires.
2. With adult help, cut slits all around the edges of the cardboard. Cut the slits about 1" (3 cm) deep and space them about 3" (8 cm) apart.
3. Cut pieces of yarn or other fibers into 12' (4 m) lengths for easy weaving and wrapping.

Hint: Roll yarn and fibers into balls, which will unroll easily and are more easily managed than skeins or extra long pieces.

4. Tie a knot on the end of the yarn. Pull the yarn into one of the slits so the unknotted end comes out on the front of the cardboard. (The knot stays on the back of the cardboard.) Drag the yarn across the front of the board to another slit of choice.
5. Loop around the edge of the slit and come back through a different slit, also on the front. Now cross over the board again, repeating the looping through a slit. If the yarn runs out, tie a new piece to the old piece and keep on wrapping and weaving.
6. Weave and wrap until the cardboard is filled to the satisfaction of the artist(s).
7. Tie the last end of yarn to another in a good knot to finish.

VARIATIONS

Weave and wrap other materials into the design, such as strips of torn fabric, rick-rack, curling ribbon, hair ribbon, and so on.

MATERIALS

heavy cardboard
knife (adult only) or scissors
fibers, yarn, strips of fabric, sewing trims

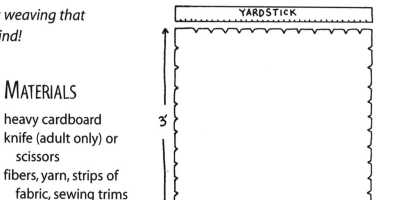

YARDSTICK

3'

CLOSE-UP

Gradient Chromatic Mosaic

Using colorful squares of cut-up cereal boxes, form a color gradient work of art that flows from one color value to another, from light to dark, across the poster board.

MATERIALS

cereal boxes or other colorful lightweight boxes

scissors (or paper cutter, adult only)

5 or more boxes

glue

big piece of cardboard or poster board

PROCESS

1. Cut cereal boxes or other lightweight cardboard into hundreds of 2" (5 cm) squares. An adult can use a paper cutter to cut many squares quickly.
2. Separate the squares into different boxes by color value, that is, by lightness or darkness of color. For example, you might have white, beige, and gray as values of white, or red, red-orange, and pink as values of red.
3. When the colors are separated, line up the boxes from the lightest color values to the darkest, in one long line.
4. Start by gluing the lightest squares edge to edge on the poster board. When the lightest colors are glued, move to a slightly darker color. When those are gone, add the next darker color, until all the colors are used from the very lightest to the very darkest.

Hint: When gluing squares down, push the straight edges of the squares right up next to each other. Squares can be glued in long lines or other patterns, but snugged right up one to another.

5. Look at the mosaic, flowing from light to dark! How beautiful!

VARIATIONS

Cut up photographs into squares and make a polychromatic mosaic like above.

Use ceramic tiles, broken pottery or dishes, or plastic tiles to make mosaics.

Make mosaics on each side of a cardboard box, and hang it from one corner.

Group Clay Sculpture

There is nothing like the feel of smooth, cool clay. Clay is relaxing, and promotes imagination, creativity, and exploration. Provide artists with a few pottery tools, clay, space, and lots of time to create.

PROCESS

1. Each artist will need about 1/2 pound of clay (230 g).
2. Artists gather around the plywood base. Working together with individual mounds of clay, build and create a joined big group clay sculpture of either a random abstract design, or something more pictorial and realistic.
3. Use wet sponges for smoothing the clay. Use pottery tools for creating textures or straight edges. Explore and have fun! If it doesn't look just so, smash it down and start over again.
4. Add to the sculpture over the course of several days (dried clay can be moistened with sponges dipped in water).
5. When the artists agree that the masterpiece is complete, let dry until a soft, dusty color.
6. When dry, paint the clay work with tempera paint, if desired.

Hint: Because this clay was not fired in a kiln, it is not permanent like pottery you might use for dishes or planter pots. This is simply dried clay.

MATERIALS

many hands and imaginations
wet potters clay (often called Moist Clay or Earth Clay)
large plywood base, about 3' x 3' (1 m x 1 m)
small containers of water
sponges
pottery tools (see list)
tempera paint, optional
paintbrushes, optional

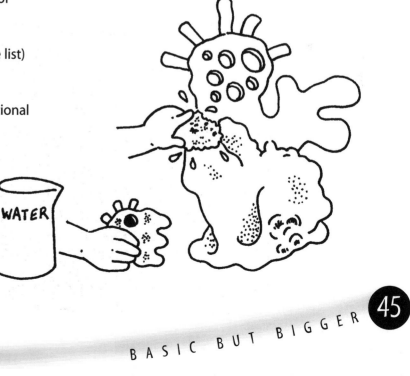

POTTERY TOOLS TO TRY

craft sticks	scoring tools
flat sticks	spatulas
forks	sponges
knives	wooden dowels
lengths of broom sticks	Think up your own ideas!

Stenciled Sheet

Decorate a bed sheet with fabric paint and stencils. When the stencils are peeled away, lasting designs remain to be enjoyed for many nights of sweet dreams.

PEEL THE PROTECTIVE BACKING....

MATERIALS

plastic sheet or news-
   paper
duct tape
white sheet or bed
   linens
self-adhesive vinyl,
   such as Contac
   paper
scissors
fabric paint in
   containers
paintbrushes

PROCESS

1. Cover a table or wall with a sheet of plastic or newspaper.
2. Tape the white sheet to the table or to a wall with heavy duct tape. Keep the sheet stretched tight, if possible.
3. Cut out shapes from the vinyl. The shapes can be random or form a picture or scene. Consider making vinyl borders too.
Hint: Cut letters as they would be read, not backwards.
4. Peel the protective backing from the vinyl shapes. Stick them on the sheet in a random or planned design. Smooth them to remove wrinkles and bubbles.
5. Paint the fabric paint on the sheet, painting right over the vinyl stick-ons. Let the fabric paint dry.
6. Peel off the vinyl shapes and see the stenciled white spaces left behind.
7. Design one sheet, or make an entire set including pillowcases.
8. For washing instructions, read the information printed on the fabric paint container. Usually washing removes very little color, allowing for lasting enjoyment of the painted fabrics.

VARIATIONS

Stick on vinyl shapes and paint over them as above. Dry, and then peel away. Now add a second layer of shapes, overlapping the original white stencil shapes. Paint, dry, peel again. The colors will overlap and blend. This is reminiscent of batik work done with layers of wax.

Stenciled Sheet (continued)

VARIATIONS (continued)

Cut the vinyl into letters and make names, a celebration banner, or
other message.

Cut a shape from a piece of adhesive vinyl. The piece is the positive
stencil, and the hole left is the negative stencil. Make designs from
both stencils.

Create a happy birthday banner that can be used year after year.
Make one for each member of the family!

Paint and stencil other fabrics, like a tablecloth, table runner, border
for window curtains, T-shirt, and so on.

Big Big Fresco

Spread drywall mud in a large pizza box. When it's setting up but still damp, paint on the drywall mud to make a large, easy fresco (a painting on plaster). When the mud is completely dry, peel away the pizza box and display the fresco.

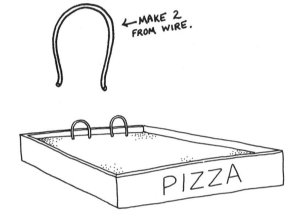

← MAKE 2 FROM WIRE.

PIZZA

PIZZA

Materials

ready-to-use drywall mud
wallpaper smoother tool or any spatula
large pizza box
2 pieces of strong wire, each about 4" (10 cm) long
tempera or watercolor paint
cups
paintbrushes, small to medium point

Process

1. Spread drywall mud with a wallpaper smoother tool or a spatula in a large pizza box to a depth of about 1" (3 cm). Make it as smooth as possible, leveling ridges and points. For even larger frescos, use larger forms
2. Bend a piece of wire to make a horseshoe-shaped loop. Repeat. Tuck the open ends of the wire pieces into the top edge of the wet mud, so they stick out about 1/2" (1.5 cm). Allow to dry in place to be used as hooks.
3. Let the mud set up for several hours until firm and hard, but still damp.

Clean-up tip: Wash drywall mud from tools outdoors. A little bit in the sink won't hurt, but too much might clog the drain.

4. Paint directly on the damp drywall mud. The paint will soak into the compound slightly while you paint.
5. When done, allow the fresco to dry completely.
6. Then peel away the pizza box so the fresco can be displayed. Hang from the looped wire hooks in the top edge of the fresco.

Variations

Spread drywall mud
    on cardboard. Let dry completely. Draw or color on the hard mud with markers, chalk, or watercolor paint.
    in a pizza box, and then stick interesting collage items into the wet mud. Let dry.

Grande Stained Glass

Do you need a magnificent stained glass decoration for your window, or would you just like to see bright colors with the sun shining through them? Make decorations for any window, large or small!

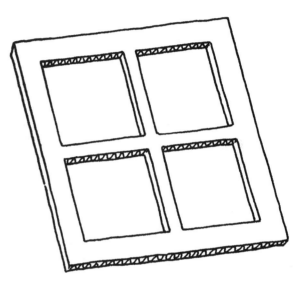

PROCESS

1. An adult prepares the cardboard with a sharp knife: Cut squares out of the cardboard, leaving "frames." (See illustration.) The cardboard will look something like a window with wax paper panes and cardboard cross frames. If desired, cut the cardboard the same size as the window you wish to decorate.
2. Cover the window openings with wax paper. Tape the wax paper on the back of the cardboard with wide shipping tape. Glue works fine too.

Hint: If the window openings are bigger than the wax paper, tape or glue sheets of wax paper together until large enough to cover the holes (use a clear tape).

3. Put newspaper or sheet of plastic on the worktable or floor. Put the cardboard window on top of it.
4. Place bowls of liquid starch next to the cardboard.
5. Cut or tear art tissue into large pieces and shapes. Some artists work in a random way, others work toward a pictorial scene or planned design. A "quilted" design can also be effective.
6. Paint the tissue onto the wax paper with liquid starch or thinned white glue. Overlap the pieces so the wax paper is completely filled in. Pieces of tissue may also be placed over each other (for example, a star in the middle of a circle). Paint and soak each piece of tissue with starch. Work until all the wax paper is covered with colorful art tissue designs.

MATERIALS

cardboard
knife (adult only)
wax paper
wide shipping tape or glue
newspaper or sheet of plastic
liquid starch or thinned glue
bowls
art tissue, whole sheets or large scraps
scissors, optional
brushes or sponges
push pins or tape

Grande Stained Glass (continued)

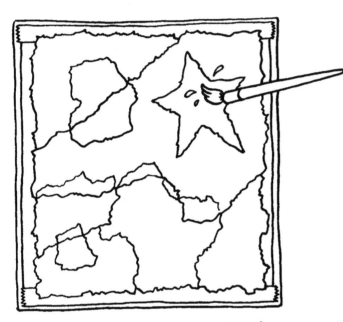

WAXED PAPER TAPED TO WINDOW

7. Let the tissue dry overnight. The next day, hoist up the cardboard window design and place it in the chosen window. Push pins or tape can hold it in place. See the sun shine through! When it's dark outside, leave the lights on and go outside to see the design glowing into the night.

VARIATIONS

Make panels that tell a story. Line them up in a big picture window.
Create Christmas decorations or other holiday ideas. Keep from year to year.
Work on big sheets of clear plastic wrap without cardboard. Tape the decorated plastic wrap in the window when done.

Builder's Relief Panel

Build a big panel *that shows all the great stuff you can collect from a construction site with the builder's help. Then cover it all with drywall mud, let dry, and paint! It's like building a work of art!*

PROCESS

1. This art project is great to do right at a construction site (with permission from the builder, of course!), but if this isn't possible, bring everything back inside.
2. Spread a big board on the ground. Begin nailing wood scraps to the board. Be careful that nails don't go through and out the other side of the board.
   Hint: Adults should supervise this step closely, and everyone should wear safety glasses.
3. Cover the board with a flat structure, or build it high.
4. When done, open the tub of drywall mud. Spread the white "mud" all over the wood scraps with the spreaders. Be careful of any nails poking out. Cover everything until the entire sculpture is white. Then let dry overnight, at least 24 hours. The structure should be moved indoors or to a sheltered area to dry.
5. With house painting brushes, dip into the paint and paint the structure. Paint will go on nice and smooth over the drywall mud. Leave some of the sculpture white, if you like. Paint and paint. Then let dry in a covered area.
6. Leave the sculpture on the construction site for the builders, carpenters, plumbers, and electricians to enjoy, or move it to a display area at home, school, or the nearest art gallery!

MATERIALS

construction site (or other work space)
large board
wood scraps, lumber scraps, board scraps, drywall scraps
hammer and nails (use caution)
safety glasses
tub of drywall mud
spreaders, spatulas, or pieces of cardboard
leftover paint or any paint
house painting brushes

51

Chapter 3

All Kinds of Brushes

⊙ ① ✎ Other-Than-Brushes Paintings

Dip, drag, press, and whap things found in the kitchen, garage, play room, and yard. Anything goes! Make prints, paintings, paint-rubbings, texture prints, or devise an experi-mental art experience. Check out the list on pages 55-56 for ideas.

MATERIALS

tempera paint
shallow, flat pans
wooden back
  massager
paper

BACK MASSAGER NOT-SO-MESSY PAINTING

PROCESS

1. Pour tempera paint into a shallow, flat container.
2. Roll the wooden wheeled back massager through paint. (A back massager looks like a wooden car with a U-shaped handle and four wheels.)
3. Then roll it on paper.
4. Look at the surprising design it makes!
5. Rinse when done, and save for more painting experiences.

TURKEY BASTER EXTRA-MESSY PAINTING

MATERIALS

powdered tempera paint, big piece of paper, turkey baster, container of water

PROCESS

1. Work outside.
2. Sprinkle dry tempera paint on a big sheet of paper.
3. Squeeze some water in the turkey baster.
4. Squirt it onto the paper, then let it dry.
5. Or, as a variation, fill cups with tempera paint, dip the turkey baster into the paint, and squirt at a blank piece of paper. Work outdoors and hose off any spills.

Other-Than-Brushes List

A

animals, plastic
animals/toys, plastic or rubber
    feet of
anything you can find

B

back-scrubbers, variety
balloons
balls, any variety
balls, golf
balls, Koosh
baskets, plastic strawberry
bath puffs, mesh
bellows, small
berry baskets
Bingo daubers
blocks
body parts
boots
bottle caps
bottles, long neck Coca-Cola
bottles, pump
bottles, spray
bottles, squeeze
brayers
brooms, child size or full size
brushes, house painting types
brushes, toilet bowl (clean ones,
    of course)
bubble wrap

bumpy things, glued to cardboard,
    paper towel tubes, or gloves
buttons

C

cans, dipped in paint make nice
    circles
cardboard, pieces
cardboard, with string glued on it
carpet and upholstery samples
cars, toy
cars, with wheels
caster cups
casters
checkers
clothesline
clothespins
combs
containers with shaker tops
cookie cutters
corks
corn cobs, dried
craft sticks
crayons, wax
crayons, paint
crepe paper

D

dandelions
deodorant bottles
dishwashing brushes
dominoes

E

egg cartons
eyedroppers

F

fabrics, different textures
feather dusters
film canisters
fingers, hands, toes, feet
flex tube
flowers
foam, pieces of
foil balls
forks
funnels

G

gadgets
gelatin molds
gloves
go on a hunt in the garage, kitchen,
    at garage sales, outdoors
golf balls
grip sheets, non-skid
gutter guard, plastic

H

hair rollers
hair, paint with own

I

ice cubes

J

jar lids

K

keys
kitchen tool, any
kitchen utensils
knobs

L

lattice panel
leaves
lids, from jars, containers, bottles

M

marbles
markers, dried out
mashers
meat tenderizers
molds
mops
muffin tins

N

newspaper, crumpled
nylon stockings

P

paint rollers
paintbrushes, big ones for houses
panty hose, foot filled with sand
paper cups
paper towel tubes
pine cones
pine needles
pipettes
plastic lids
plastic wrap, crumpled
plungers
poker chips
popsicle sticks
potato mashers

Q

Q-tips

R

rolling pin with fabric or yarn
   wrapped around
rolling pins
rubber bait worms

rubber bands, around blocks
rubber bands, grouped together
   and tied
rubber bands, on paint roller
rubber stamps, old

S

scouring pads
screws, big-headed
scrubbies
seashells
shoes
soap holders with soft bumps
soap holders with suction cups
socks filled with sand
spatulas
sponges, cut up or full size
sponges, in shapes
spools, old thread
spoons
spray bottles
sprayer, Hudson
springs
squeeze bottles
sticks
strawberry baskets, plastic mesh
straws
string or yarn
Styrofoam, grocery trays/meat trays

T

tile spacers
toothbrushes
toy cars
toys, any with wheels
toys, broken parts of
trowel, flooring
trowel, margin
trowel, thinset
trowel, wall

V

vinyl tiles
W
wallpaper paste brush
wallpaper seam roller
wallpaper smoothing brush
washers
weather stripping, self-adhesive
   foam
wood scraps
wooden carpentry rosettes and trim
   accents
worms, rubber bait

Y

yarn, general varieties
yarn, glued around paper towel
   tube

Find Your Own Painting Tools ⊛ ① ✎

Take a field trip to the hardware store to find interesting and unusual things for painting ideas. Some inexpensive favorites are highlighted in this remarkably artistic and gratifying painting exploration.

PROCESS

1. Go to the hardware store and search for cool stuff to use with paint. Some things will be good for dragging through paint to make patterns and textures. Other things will be used more like brushes. And still other things will be used to make prints. Select a few to keep with the paint supplies.
2. Spread out the paper.
3. Put the paint in shallow containers and place it at the edges of the paper.
4. Explore the interesting hardware tools making prints, textures, and painting. Try new painting techniques and see what happens.
5. Rinse the new painting tools and keep for an art experience on another day.

MATERIALS

stuff from a hardware store (see list)
paper, any kind
tempera paint
shallow containers
pail or dishpan with clean water

STUFF FROM THE HARDWARE STORE TO TRY

caster cups
extention springs
lattice panels
non-shed grippers
notched flooring trowel
self-adhesive foam weather stripping

thinset trowel
vinyl tiles
wallpaper smoothing brush or paste brush
washers
wood trim accents

Pine Bough Painting

Painting with pine boughs or evergreen branches goes with the month of December, but can be done anytime of the year. Free clippings are yours for the asking at Christmas tree lots. What a nostalgic fragrance!

MATERIALS

large sheets of paper
tape
tempera paint
large shallow
    containers
pine boughs or ever-
    green branches
gardening gloves,
    optional

PROCESS

1. Tape *big* pieces of paper to a wall or table.
2. Put paint in *big* semi-shallow containers to an inch (3 cm) or so in depth. Have more paint on hand to refill containers as needed.
3. Dip a pine bough in paint and then brush onto the paper, using the branch like a large paintbrush. If desired, use gardening gloves to keep hands clean and sap-free.
4. Explore other painting techniques, such as pressing, splatting, dragging, whapping, sweeping, slapping, and patting with the pine boughs.
5. Continue filling the same piece of paper or use a new sheet.
6. The more they are used, the more branches and boughs will perfume the air with a wonderful fragrance.

VARIATIONS

For those who celebrate Christmas, paint with several shades of green on white butcher paper; then cut the paper into the shape of a tree. Hang the "tree" on the wall and decorate it with some hand-painted "ornaments."
Collect lots of branches and tie them together to make a broom brush.

Loopy Roller Painting

This one's a favorite with everyone who tries it. *Wrap paint rollers with rubber bands instead of the usual fuzzy painting tube, dip in paint, and make irresistible loopy, splat designs!*

PROCESS

1. Loop rubber bands tightly on the roller cage of the paint roller.
2. Pour one color of paint in each long, flat pan.
3. Roll the paint roller in paint, then roll it on the paper.
4. Repeat the rolling in paint and rolling on paper until satisfied with the painting design.
5. To dry, set aside when complete.
6. Bring in fresh paper, and continue as desired.

VARIATIONS

Wrap rubber bands on a fuzzy paint roller tube.
Work on paper that is taped to the wall, like rolling paint on a wall.
Keep some rubber bands in loops, and cut some others so the ends stick out.
Use string, yarn, or rag strips instead of rubber bands.

MATERIALS

3"-5" (8 cm-15 cm)
  paint rollers
large rubber bands
tempera paint
long, flat paint pans
paper

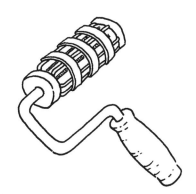

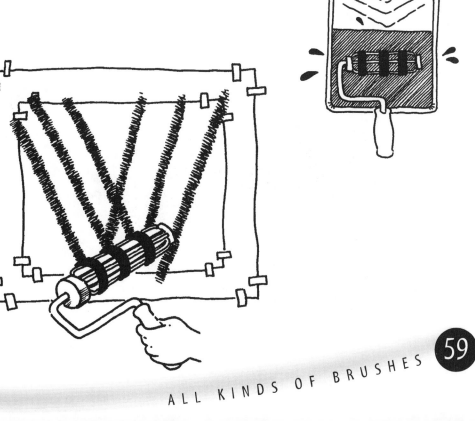

59

Mops and Brooms Painting

Mops and brooms can be extraordinary paintbrushes for artwork that will sweep you away! Using child-sized cleaning tools, paint a mural on a long sheet of paper stretched out on the floor.

Materials

tempera paint
plastic dishpans
butcher paper or craft
  paper
newspaper
tape
child-size mops and
  brooms
buckets of clear water

Process

1. Pour several different colors of paint into separate plastic dishpans to about 1/2" (1.5 cm) deep. Refill the tubs as needed.
2. Spread out large sheets of paper on the ground. If working indoors, spread lots of newspaper out first to protect the floor, and be sure to tape the paper down so it won't wiggle.
3. Dip a mop or broom into the paint and then paint with it on the paper.
Hint: Adult-size mops and brooms work well too, but are harder to handle.
4. Repeat the dipping and sweeping steps until satisfied with the painting.
5. Have more paper on hand to make a second or third painting when each one is complete.
6. When done, allow the painting to dry where it is or move it to a spot out of the way of traffic. Meanwhile, swish mops and brooms in buckets of clear water to rinse.

Variations

Paint with other unusual brush-type tools, including:
  dishwashing sponges on plastic handle
  dishwashing brushes
  long-handled squeegees
  adult-size brooms or mops with shortened handles
  any variety of scrub brushes
  whisk brooms.
Tape paper to a wall, fence, or garage door instead of spreading it on the ground.

Drippy Daubers

Squeeze a sponge into the toe of a child's old sock and tie it closed. Then daub the sock in paint, just like a huge Bingo marker! Make one for every color of the rainbow.

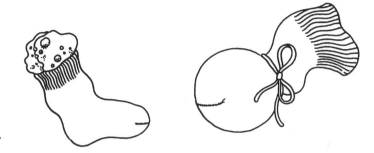

PROCESS

1. Stuff a kitchen sponge into the toe of a child's old sock. If possible, make seven socks with seven sponges for the seven colors of the rainbow.
2. Tie the sock closed with heavy yarn or string. Tie the sock very tight.
3. Set each sock in a pan of paint.
4. Paint on a piece of cardboard placed upright or paint on paper. Place newspaper under to catch drips.
5. Press the paint-filled socks on the paper, daubing and dripping the paint down.
6. Re-dip in other colors, to mix colors right on the dauber. Or only put daubers back into their own colors so no mixing occurs on the dauber.
7. Try writing or drawing with the daubers too. Making polka-dots is easy!
8. When completely finished with the activity, daubers can be soaked in water, and then squeezed and cleaned under the faucet. Some artists really enjoy watching the colors mix and wash down the drain of a white sink.

VARIATIONS

Be a two-fisted dauber, one in each hand.
Make a bouquet of daubers, and make daubing prints with four or more colors at a time.

MATERIALS

kitchen sponges
child's old socks
pieces of heavy yarn or string
tempera paint
pans for paint
scissors
cardboard or paper
newspaper
tape

61

Streamers Artwork

Crepe paper streamers have a surprising amount of color packed into them. Tie wet streamers to ankles, and shuffle across the paper, making designs. Wear old socks unless you want the brightest ankles in town!

Materials

old socks
big length of butcher
   or craft paper
tape
shallow pans
water
crepe paper streamers
scissors
rubber gloves, optional

Process

1. Remove shoes and put on old socks. Roll up pants, too!
2. Spread the paper on the floor. Tape it down to prevent scuffing and wiggling.
3. Fill the shallow pans with about 1" (3 cm) of water. Place shallow pans of water next to the paper.
4. Cut crepe paper streamers into 3' (1 m) lengths. Dip the ends of the streamers in each tub of water. Remove when lightly soaked.
Clean-up tip: Fingers will pick up color, so wear rubber gloves if you want clean hands.
5. Tie a streamer to each ankle.
6. Stand on the edge of the paper and walk in a gentle scuffling or scooting motion across the paper, dragging the streamers behind. Experiment with different movements to allow the streamers to paint designs on the paper.
7. Change colors and add more streamer designs to the paper.
8. When done, streamers can be discarded or saved for other paper art projects (make homemade paper, page 94). Socks can be washed or left as is for other art projects.

Variations

Hang a long strip of fabric from a belt and onto the paper like a very long tail. Dip the tail in paint, and drag the tail across the paper to make "tail paintings." Wear old pants and old socks.
Soak crepe paper in bowls of water until the water is heavily colored. Paint with brushes on white paper with the crepe paper "paint."

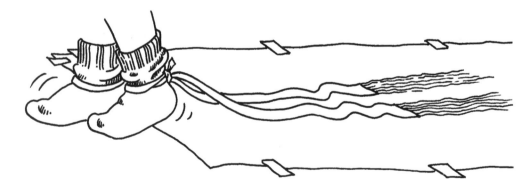

Squeegee Scraping

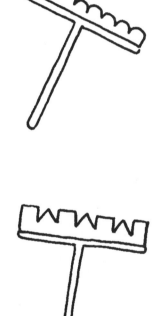

Create art scrapers from rubber squeegees. The artists design the squeegees and the adults cut them. Artists just love scrapers that make interesting lines and designs in their paintings, but because this book is about Big and Messy, let's make some BIG scrapers!

Preparing the Squeegees

squeegees for shower, car window, or basic window size
kitchen shears, scissors, or other sharp knife (adult only)
The artist picks the designs such as fringe, wavy, toothy, or squared-
   off. See illustrations for suggestions. The adult cuts designs into
   the edge of the rubber squeegee. Make sure the cuts in the rubber edge of the squeegee are fairly deep and spaced apart so the
   ridges made in paint will show.

Puff Paint Recipe

4 cups (1 L) flour
4 cups (1 L) water
4 cups (1 L) salt
3 tablespoons (45 mL) powdered tempera paint or just use less
   liquid tempera
bowl and spoon
Mix the first four ingredients in a bowl. Make one big batch of one
   color, or divide an uncolored batch into several smaller bowls that
   can be individually colored with a little paint mixed in each one.

Squeegee Scraping (continued)

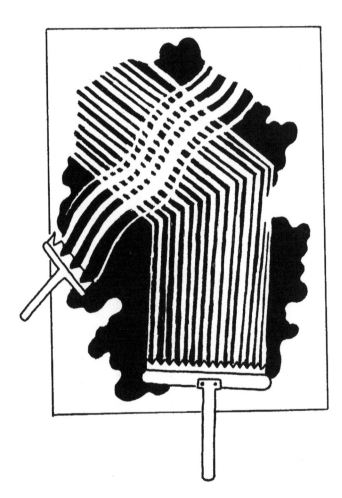

MATERIALS

puff paint (see recipe-
   on page 63)
spoon
posterboard
pre-made squeegee
   scrapers (see direc-
   tions on page 63)

PROCESS

1. Drop big blobs of puff paint on the poster board.
2. Begin by fingerpainting on the poster board to spread out the paint.
3. Use the squeegee scrapers to drag designs and textures through the paint, adding dimension and interest.
4. Let the paint design dry on the poster board. It will dry hard, puffy, and sparkly (from the salt).

VARIATIONS

Cut cardboard rectangles into "combs" like the squeegees.
Use regular fingerpaint on butcher paper.
Work directly on a smooth tabletop with fingerpaint. Wash off when done.
Skip adding any color to the puff paint and work on dark colored poster board with uncolored puff paint.

Body Part Prints

Stamping with different parts of the body? Yes! This is a truly big and messy art activity that is especially for naturally messy (creative!) artists, and also gives more timid souls an opportunity to explore at their own pace.

PROCESS

1. Consider doing this project outside on a summer day with lots of water and towels for cleanup and a change of clothes on hand. Wear old play clothes or old bathing suits. For indoor creating, be prepared! Cover the work area with plastic sheeting or newspapers.
2. To make the stamp pad, fold the old hand towels into thirds. Folded towels will be about 7" x 14" (18 cm x 35 cm), in three layers. Soak each towel with tempera paint and place in a shallow pan.
3. To make the body part prints, press a body part (fingers, hand, arm, foot, shin, cheek, chin, even a bottom!) on the pad and then on the paper. Make as many body prints as desired.
4. Set the paper aside, and allow the prints to dry while making additional ones.

Clean-up tip: Artists can rinse themselves in the soapy water, hose off, and dry with old towels. An additional bath or shower may be needed later.

VARIATIONS

Attach the paper to the wall or large easel and make prints.

Trace an artist's body on the paper and let him or her add the prints to fill in. An older artist can create himself or herself on the paper without an outline.

MATERIALS

old hand towels
tempera paint
shallow pans
large sheets of paper

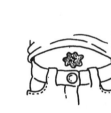

FOLD INTO THIRDS

SOAK IN TEMPERA PAINT

ELBOW

← BELLY BUTTON!

Skate-N-Paint

Roll out a long sheet of butcher paper and roll your way from end to end *lying on a skateboard with painted hands. Caution: This activity causes laughter!*

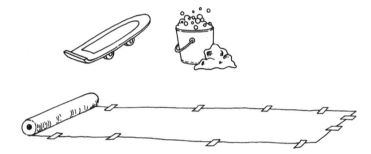

MATERIALS

open area of floor or
   outdoor area
newspapers, optional
butcher paper or craft
   paper
tape
tempera paint
non-tip containers
paintbrushes or
   sponge brushes
skateboard
2 or more artists
soapy bucket of water
   and old towels

PROCESS

1. If necessary, protect the art area with newspaper.
2. Roll out a long sheet of butcher paper on the floor. Tape corners here and there along the way to keep paper from wiggling.
3. Put paint in flat, non-tip containers. Place the paint and brushes at the beginning of the paper.
   Clean-up tip: Mix tempera paint with a little liquid dish soap for easy cleanup.
4. The artist sits or lies tummy down on the skateboard and sticks out his or her bare hands (or feet!).
5. Another artist paints both palms with tempera paint.
6. Roll down the long paper, pushing with hands, and leaving prints along the way. Wash hands in the soapy bucket of water and dry with the old towel before starting off on new prints. Washing, however, is *not* required.
7. For the next artist's turn, change paint colors but use the same sheet of paper. (Don't be surprised when wheels get painty too.)

VARIATIONS

At the end of the paper, turn around and roll back, making tracks through the painted areas.

Sit on the skateboard with a friend; dip all four feet in paint and work together to get to the end.

Dip the skateboard in a large, shallow pan of paint before you begin rolling to get prints from the wheels.

Drive trikes or bikes through paint and onto paper.

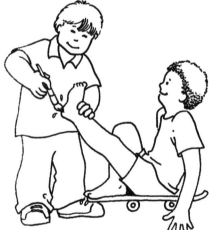

No-Hands Painting

Try something different—paint with anything but hands! Use Velcro to attach paintbrushes to various parts of the body, and paint away. It's fun to figure out just how and where to attach the brushes and even more fun to maneuver the brushes to paint.

PROCESS

1. Cut lengths of Velcro strips 12"-18" (30 cm-45 cm), or use Velcro straps available at sport, bike, or hardware stores.
2. Pour tempera paint in non-tip pans and spread out the brushes beside the pans.

Hint: Adults can hot glue brushes to the Velcro straps for sturdy painting tools.

3. Tape paper to a wall or table.
4. Strap brushes onto arms, legs, feet, elbows, wherever you want. You decide! Part of the creativity with this activity will be the dipping and painting.
5. Dip brushes into paint and paint on the paper.

VARIATIONS

Collect other items to paint with instead of brushes:
   small paint rollers
   feather duster
   dish scrubber on long handle
   spatula
   back scrubber, sponge, or puff on long handle
   broom or mop, child-size
   see list on pages 55-56, Other-Than-Brushes List.

MATERIALS

Velcro and scissors or
   Velcro straps
tempera paint
non-tip flat pans
paintbrushes
big sheets of paper
tape

Rope Painting

Take string painting to a grand scale! With lengths of rope dipped in paint, create giant swirls and sliding strokes of paint on large sheets of butcher paper.

MATERIALS

newspapers
large sheets of butcher paper or craft paper
dishpans
tempera paint
3'-4' (1 m-1.5 m) lengths of rope or cord

PROCESS

1. Place a large sheet of paper on the floor on top of newspapers, or outside on the ground.
2. Fill dishpans with tempera paint to about 1" (3 cm) deep and place beside the paper. Use one dishpan for each color of paint.
3. Tie a loop handle in one end of each length of rope.
4. Place two or three ropes in each color of paint with handles hanging over the edges of the pans.
5. Pick up a rope by its handle, and then drag it across the paper, making paint designs where the rope touches.
6. Another idea is to fold the paper in half, then open. Arrange a paint-filled length of rope on the paper with the handle hanging off the paper. Fold the paper over the rope. Several artist press their hands and arms over the folded paper to slightly hold back the rope, while another artist pulls the rope out of the folded paper. Unfold.
7. When satisfied with the design, set aside to dry in an out-of-the-way spot, and create more rope designs. Ropes can be rinsed, dried, and used again for art projects.

VARIATIONS

Use ropes made of different materials, such as cotton, hemp, jute, or plastic.
Tie objects to the rope along its length, such as corks, hair curlers, cotton balls, or ribbon streamers.

Dancing Beads

An artwork that feels like marionettes dancing on painty toes before your eyes!

ART PROCESS

1. Tie each bead to a foot-long (30 cm) piece of string. Make five, one for each finger of one hand.
2. Tape one string to each finger on one hand.
3. Dip the beads into the paint in the bowl, and then dangle and dance the beads on the paper.
   Hint: It will look like a string puppet.
4. When the paint fades, dip in a new color or the same one, and continue to paint.

VARIATIONS

Paint on a sloped surface so the beads roll down the incline on the paper.

Hang a different item from each string on a finger.

Work with both hands at once!

Tape markers to fingers, like drawing with very long fingernails.

MATERIALS

5 strings, each 1' (30 cm) long

5 heavy beads (washers or buttons work too)

tape

bowls of tempera paint

large sheet of paper

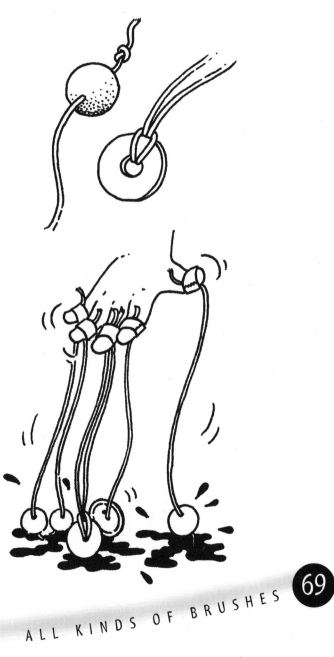

69

Rag Print Wall Border

Create a stylish border with a scrunched-up rag dipped in washable latex paint! Rags make beautiful prints, and a border is just messy enough to attract young decorators but with paint still in reasonable control.

PAINTER'S PAPER

THIS IS FIRST LINE OF TAPE. YOUR "STRAIGHT EDGE".

PAINTER'S PAPER

MATERIALS

pencil

yardstick or measuring tape

painter's masking tape (look for the blue, easy pull-off kind)

painter's masking paper (looks like lightweight brown craft paper, comes on a roll)

latex paint (choose a semi-gloss color)

paint roller plastic pan (the sloped, bumpy kind)

rubber gloves or plastic gloves

rags, like old T-shirts, about 12" x 12" (30 cm x 30cm)

paper

old clothes, old shoes, and rags for wiping hands

PROCESS

Painting a border around a room requires adult interaction, assistance, and supervision from start to finish. The artist will make the rag prints independently.

TO PREPARE THE BORDER FOR PAINTING (SEE ILLUSTRATIONS FOR HELP.)

1. Mark the area to be painted, using a yardstick or measuring tape to measure 3' up from the floor.
2. Use a pencil to make a dot every few inches all the way across the wall.
3. Put a continuous piece of masking tape from one dot to the other.
4. Measure 5" (or 8" or any other size) from the masking tape line.
5. Again, make pencil dots every few inches across the wall.
6. Put a continuous piece of masking tape from one dot to another.
7. The space left is the space that will be painted.
8. Next tape painter's paper to the masking tape border to protect the wall on both sides. Use long lines of tape to attach the paper to the tape that is already on the wall.
9. You're ready to make rag prints!

Rag Print Wall Border (continued)

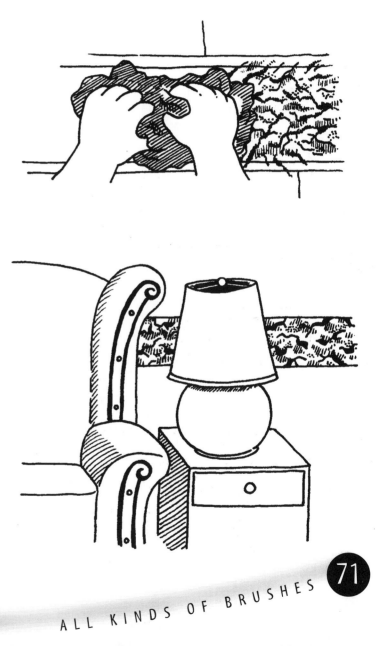

To Make the Rag Prints

1. First practice printing on extra paper to see how it all works. Pour the mixed paint into the paint pan and set the pan on the big template to protect the floor. Put on gloves. Dip a scrunched-up rag into the paint a little bit. Press a print on the paper. Look at the print. Decide if you need to use more or less paint, make more wrinkles in the rag, etc.
2. Now dip the rag into the paint again and press on the border area of the wall. Daub a few prints, and then re-dip. Make rag prints all around the entire room in the taped border area.

Hint: A half-gallon should be enough for a 10′ x 10′ (3 m x 3 m) room's border. Have the paint thoroughly mixed at the paint store. One color is a good start for beginning painters, but you can choose two colors if you want to print a second color over the first.

3. You've done it! Would you like a second color over the first? Let the first coat of paint dry until it is at least tacky or almost dry. Completely dry is fine too.
4. Now repeat the process using a second color and a new rag print over the first.
5. Let the border dry overnight.
6. Pull the masking tape and paper from the wall and discard in the recycle bin. (You could save it for making a Dino Sculpture page, 118.)
7. What a great look! Would you like to print an entire wall, not just a border? Maybe another day! Now it's time to clean up as you would for any house-painting job. Rags can be discarded.

Cheerful note: Latex paint is washable.

Variation

Create a border at ceiling height.

Rag print an entire wall.

Experiment with other fabrics or materials to make prints, such as a sponge, a block of wood, or a mesh dish scrubber.

BIG MESSY ART

Chapter 4

Mixtures and Moosh

BIG Basic Art Dough

Take art dough from an individual tabletop activity to a new dimension! It's great for large groups, resourceful small groups, or inventive individuals.

MATERIALS

10 lb. (4.5 kg) flour
10 cups (2.5 L) salt
17 cups (4.25 L) water
big plastic tub
sheet of plywood or
    particle board
paint and paint-
    brushes

PROCESS

1. Place flour, salt, and water in a big plastic tub.
Note: This recipe can be halved for a reduced but still very large amount of dough.
2. Mix the art dough with hands until smooth and pliable. (This takes about 10 minutes.) Roll up those sleeves!
3. Place the dough on the plywood or particle board.
4. The artists use the art dough to create a group sculpture of any design or theme on the particle board. An individual can also create his or her own sculpture.
5. Let the sculpture dry.
6. Paint the dry masterpiece with tempera paints or any paints on hand.
Hints: To keep extra dough soft, cover with clear plastic wrap secured with tape. This activity is great for out-of-doors, which assists with drying time.

VARIATIONS

To make an individually inspired group sculpture, children make individual sculptures, and then after they dry, glue them together on one base or board.
To make colored dough, add watercolor or tempera paint or food coloring to the water when mixing the dough.
To make textured dough, add coffee grounds or sand during the mixing stage.

Confetti Paint

Fall is a time for brilliant, colorful changes perfect for appreciation through an easy art idea. Here's a way to preserve some of that color in a unique relaxed painting activity that captures the shine of supple autumn leaves.

PROCESS

1. Gather fall leaves. Look for many different colors.
2. Crumble or tear colorful autumn leaves into small bits. Keep like colors together or mix and match.
3. Gently stir the leaf bits into the glue in a small bowl. If sorting leaves by color, have a separate mixing cup for each color.
4. Dip a paintbrush into the new autumn confetti paint and make glossy fall pictures on heavy paper.
5. Dry at least overnight or until glue dries clear.

VARIATIONS

Glue the leaf paint on paper cut into leaf shapes.

Keep the leaves whole. Glue them onto paper and then paint over the leaf with clear glue for a decoupage effect.

Use torn bits of flower petals, weeds and grasses, and/or spring leaves.

Paint this glossy fall paint on a small wooden box or plain cardboard gift box.

MATERIALS

fall leaves
white glue
small bowls or other
  containers
paintbrushes
heavy paper or light-
  weight cardboard

Mud Dough

Mudpies are a traditional childhood aesthetic experience not to be missed by any! Take the ingredients of mudpies (yes, mud and water!) one step further and concoct a pliable dough for modeling fun.

MATERIALS

small bucket or large bowl
2 cups (500 mL) "clean" mud
2 cups (500 mL) sand
1/2 cup (125 mL)) salt
water
measuring cups
old wooden spoon to mix

PROCESS

1. In a small bucket or large mixing bowl, mix together 2 cups (500 mL) mud, 2 cups (500 mL) sand, 1/2 cup (125 mL) salt, and enough water to make it pliable.

Hint: Recipe can be doubled or tripled for larger groups or bigger projects.

2. Mix with an old wooden spoon, or mix by hand.
3. Turn out the dough on a suitable work surface and model as with any dough. This activity can be done outside or inside on lots of newspapers.
4. Although sculptures do not keep, the fun of exploring mud as dough will capture the interest of the most reticcent artist.

VARIATIONS

Add other ingredients to the dough, such as chopped grasses or bits of leaves.

This dough works well as the base for building a pretend garden in a baking pan, using twigs for trees, pebble pathways, and pools of water made with foil.

Mud Dough (continued)

EXPERIMENTAL MUD PAINT

Mix "clean" powdery dirt with regular cooking oil. How do you measure? By experimenting! Mix a shovel full of dirt in a bucket, add some oil, and stir until the texture of thick cream. Paint on a big flat rock or some paper. No oil? Use water. No dirt? Use commercial clay mixed with water to make mud. Different kinds of soils and clays will produce different colors of paint. Try painting on paper or cardboard. Fabric stretched on a board is fun to paint on too.

SLIMO FINGERMUD

Mix "clean" dirt and water to make mud in a bucket or bowl. Add liquid starch and dishwashing detergent, mixing well until the consistency of fingerpaint. There are no perfect measurements, so you must experiment to create a nice consistency. Use like fingerpaint on paper, fabric, cardboard, or bare tabletops. Keep a bottle of water nearby to thin the paint while using.

Goop and Funny Putty

No book about big, messy art would be complete without two traditional recipes: Goop and Funny Putty. These recipes have been around for quite awhile, but they're just too big and too messy—and too wonderful—to omit.

MATERIALS

1 lb. box (450 g) cornstarch
plastic dishpan
2 1/2 cups (600 mL) water
measuring cup
play tools, like spoon, cups, sand shovel, kitchen utensils
food coloring

GOOP

PROCESS

1. Dump the entire box of cornstarch into a plastic dishpan.
2. Add the water and mix by hand.
3. Mix and play in the Goop, noting its strange liquid-to-solid-to-liquid behavior.
4. Add other toys and utensils to the exploration.
5. Add drops of food coloring, and mix the colors in by hand or with tools. You could mix small separate cups of colored Goop, and then mix them all together in one big tub.
6. Explore the possibilities!

Clean-up tip: To discard used Goop, thin the mixture with water until it is like milk. Wash it down the drain.

Goop and Funny Putty (continued)

FUNNY PUTTY

measuring cups and spoons
2 teaspoons (10 mL) Borax
1/3 cup (80 mL) water
1-cup measuring cup for dissolving Borax
2 cups (500 mL) white glue
1 3/4 cups (420 mL) water

mixing bowl and spoon
food coloring, optional
play tools, like spoons, forks, dull knives, and
   kitchen utensils
Sunday funnies, comic book, or newspaper
container that closes

PROCESS

1. Mix the 2 teaspoons (10 mL) Borax and 1/3 cup (80 mL) of water
   in the one-cup measuring cup. Let the Borax dissolve completely.
2. Mix the 2 cups (500 mL) glue and 1 3/4 cup (420 mL) water in the mixing bowl.
   Add the Borax mixture. Stir well with a spoon or hands.
3. The mixture will suddenly, magically, begin to glomb together. Keep
   kneading the mixture in the bowl. Some moisture may remain, but
   ignore it.
4. Turn the Funny Putty mixture out on the table. Use kitchen tools and toys
   to explore the Funny Putty. Try picking up a picture from the funnies or a comic book or
   the newspaper.
6. When exploration is complete, Funny Putty can be stored in a closed container or plastic
   zipper-closure baggie for about two weeks, or until it begins to have a strong odor.

VARIATIONS

Make plain Funny Putty, and during the kneading and mixing step, add a few drops of food
   coloring. Watch the color mix in.
Place in candy molds (cookie cutters work too) to see the putty form itself to fit the shape.
Press fingers or tools into the putty. Watch the designs disappear.

Hanging Glue Squiggles

Squiggle white glue on wax paper and let it dry in clear, hard shapes. After coloring the squiggle, hang from a thread overhead to sway and twirl from the air currents in the room.

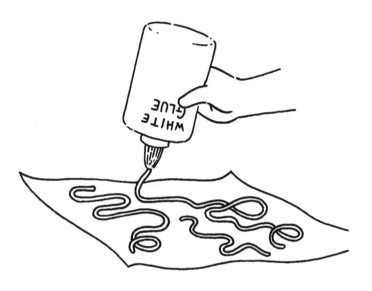

MATERIALS

wax paper
white glue in squeeze
    bottles
any bright paint
shallow dishes
paintbrushes, cotton
    balls, or sponge
    cubes
newspapers
thread
scissors
push-pins, optional

PROCESS

1. Spread a large piece of wax paper on the table.
2. Squeeze glue from the bottle onto the wax paper in squiggles, wiggles, and drizzles, all connected in a large, loopy, squiggly design. Set aside to dry for one or two days, until clear and hard.
3. Make more squiggles. Set those aside to dry too.
4. Pour paint in shallow dishes. Dip fingers, brushes, or other painting tools in the bright paint. Then spread or smear it on the dry squiggle. Use one or many colors.
5. Set aside on newspapers to dry.
6. When dry, tie a thread to each squiggle. Tie the other end of the thread to a push-pin, and push into the ceiling where the squiggle can hang and move in the air currents.

Hint: There are many ways to hang the squiggles, depending on your ceiling. You could tie several squiggles to a clothes hanger, to an overhead light, or to partitions in ceiling tiles. Squiggles could hang from a dowel or branch, or from a "seasonal tree." Hang squiggles in the window or on the wall.

VARIATIONS

Color squiggles by dipping them in a color bath in a deep container filled with food coloring or paint and water. Let drip dry briefly, and then hang from a drying rack.

Color the glue with paint or food coloring before making the squiggles. Fill squeeze bottles with different colors of glue. Mix colors on the wax paper, or use one color only.

Melted Packing Peanuts

Biodegradable packing peanuts made from cornstarch are great for packing and for gooey art projects. These packing peanuts melt with liquid and make the coolest foamy goop, 3-D art, and also make a great paste! What fun!

SIMPLE STICK AND BUILD

1. Moisten a peanut in a dish of water.
2. Stick the peanut to another peanut. Moistening the peanuts melts them slightly so they will stick together.
3. Build any sculpture shape you can imagine! Build and build as big as you want! You can even make a hat if the sculpture is formed over a plastic bowl covered with plastic wrap. Easy!

MELTED TOOTHPICK SCULPTURE

1. Put lots of toothpicks and packing peanuts on the table.
2. Build any sculpture on a big piece of cardboard by sticking toothpicks and peanuts together. If you like, you can omit the toothpicks and work with peanuts sticking to each other simply by first moistening them with a little water.
3. When the sculpture is finished, drip paint onto the peanuts from eyedroppers or pipettes. Watch the sculpture melt and dissolve, changing shape and becoming something new and surprising! Then let dry.
4. You can save this misshapen masterpiece.

Clean-up tip: Eco-Foam is safe to wash down the sink with hot water.

MATERIALS

biodegradable packing peanuts (Eco-Foam—see note on page 82)
dish of water
toothpicks
plastic bowl and plastic wrap, optional
large piece of cardboard
diluted Liquid Watercolors or any thin liquid paint
shallow cups
eyedroppers or pipettes

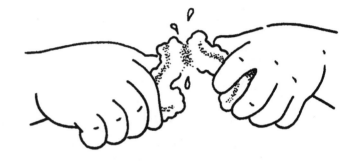

Melted Packing Peanuts (continued)

About Eco-Foam

Biodegradable packing peanuts (called Nuudles) are available from EarlyChildhood.com in pastel colors. Many companies may also use plain light-green Eco-Foam peanuts for packing orders. These plain light-green peanuts can also be purchased from shipping companies and some office supply stores that sell shipping supplies. Eco-Foam is made from puffed and dried cornstarch and is non-toxic and basically edible, though not especially appetizing. Be sure you are using cornstarch biodegradable Eco-Foam packing peanuts for this activity.

Variations

Use spray bottles with diluted Liquid Watercolors in them instead of eye droppers.

Build individual sculptures on trays or cookie sheets. They should peel away when dry.

Add plain water to Eco-Foam peanuts to make a paste.

Leftover Eco-Foam can be sprinkled outside for the birds to eat.

Fingerpainting Extravaganza Experimentia

⊙★ ①① 🖊

Make fingerpainting an artistic laboratory research project! Explore a wide variety of ingredients and materials with fingers and hands just to see what happens. Mix, moosh, spread, and smear. Discovery, learning, and fun are guaranteed!

PROCESS

1. Choose colors and materials for the experimentia. Place in pitchers or small bowls.
2. Scoop the materials directly onto paper or trays, or mix in cups first. Start with only two or three.
3. Fingerpaint with and explore the materials. Discover their properties. Have extra paper on hand. It's fun to work on a smooth table-top that can be cleaned later, but if you want to cover the table, consider using an old, clean shower curtain taped down to the table. Some artists like to work on plastic trays or cookie sheets.

   Clean-up tip: Remember to keep a bucket of warm, soapy water as well as some old towels right beside the table for easy cleanup.
4. Add more ingredients.
5. Clean up as you go, or wait until the end.
6. Enjoy making designs in the materials and discovering what can happen as they interact and combine (or don't!).

MATERIALS

materials to explore
  (see list on page 84)
pitchers or small bowls
big sheets of paper or
  trays
small pitchers of water
tongue depressors
empty containers

Fingerpainting Extravaganza Experimentia (continued)

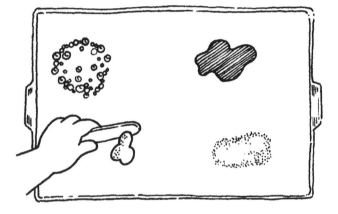

MATERIALS TO EXPLORE

bubble solution
cake flour
cooking oil
food coloring paste or liquid
hand lotion or cold cream
homemade paste (flour and water)
library paste
liquid starch
Liquid Watercolors
salt
shampoo
shaving cream
tempera paint
watercolor paint
wheat flour
wheat paste
white flour
white glue

VARIATIONS

Add simple tools to create interesting designs, such as a spatula, comb, window squeegee, ice scraper, and other kitchen utensils.

Add textures, such as coffee grounds, sand, cornmeal, sawdust, cornstarch, liquid soap, and sugar.

Add scents and extracts, such as cinnamon, vanilla extract, almond extract, orange or lemon extract, peppermint extract, perfumes, and shampoos.

Whip up some soap flakes to a foam (add paint or food coloring if you like) for a soapy, clean fingerpainting experiment.

Easy fingerpaint: Pour a puddle of liquid starch on a cookie sheet. Plunk a teaspoon of liquid or powdered tempera paint in the starch. Mix with hands and fingerpaint right on the cookie sheet. To make a print, press a piece of paper on the design and then lift. Ta-dah!

Face and Body Paint Recipes ⊙ ① ▨

Face painting comes in handy for special costume days and holidays, but can be enjoyed any time at all. These five recipes cover the gamut from face paints to one giggly tattoo paint!

Baby Lotion Face Paint

1/8 cup (30 mL) baby lotion
1/4 teaspoon (1 mL) powdered tempera paint
1 squirt liquid dishwashing soap
small dishes
make-up brushes or paintbrushes

Mix the baby lotion, powdered tempera paint, and dishwashing lotion in a small dish. Mix each color separately. Paint on the face with small, clean make-up brushes or paintbrushes. Easily removed with soap and water.
Hint: Keep any face paint away from the eyes and mouth.

Shortening-Cornstarch Face Paint

1 tablespoon (15ml) solid vegetable shortening
2 tablespoons (30ml) cornstarch
bowl and spoon
separate cups
food coloring
translucent powder and make-up pad
paintbrushes
cups

Mix solid vegetable shortening with cornstarch. Tint small portions of this creamy mixture with food coloring in separate cups, as desired. After applying the cream to the face, pat with translucent powder to "set." Remove gently with cold cream and soft tissues.

Face and Body Paint Recipes (continued)

SHORTENING-FLOUR FACE PAINT

1 tablespoon (15 mL) solid vegetable shortening
1 teaspoon (5 mL) flour
1 drop of food coloring
muffin tin
spoons

In one section of a muffin tin, mix together shortening, flour, and food coloring. Repeat to make several colors in the sections of a muffin tin. Use a finger to paint the face. Wash off with warm water and soap. Dry with soft, old towel.

THICK FACE PAINT

2 teaspoons (10 mL) solid vegetable shortening
5 teaspoons (25 mL) cornstarch
1 teaspoon (5 mL) white flour
small bowl and spoon
4 drops glycerin
food coloring
2 1/2 teaspoons (12.5 mL) cocoa, optional
paintbrushes

In a small bowl, mix vegetable shortening, cornstarch, and white flour. Add glycerin. Stir to a creamy consistency. Add any food coloring that you wish. For brown make-up, add 2 1/2 teaspoons (12.5 mL) of unsweetened cocoa instead of food coloring. Apply with a make-up brush or paintbrush. To remove, wipe face gently with cold cream and tissues or a soft, old towel. Soap and warm water also work great.

TATTOO PAINT

1 tablespoon (15 mL) cold cream
2 tablespoons (30 mL) cornstarch
1 tablespoon (15 mL) water
food coloring
mixing cups and spoons
paintbrushes

Works great! Comes off with soap and water! Also a terrific face paint. Mix cold cream, cornstarch, water, and food coloring. Stir completely. Using a clean paintbrush, create a "tattoo" anywhere on the skin.

Look for "Face Paint Plus" on page 88.

Drywall Mud Hue-Fusion

Drywall mud is cheap and *perfect for use in the art of mixing and blending colors that will dry to a rock hard consistency.*

Process

1. To begin, spread some mud on a piece of matte board. Cover the entire piece of board until it is white all over. Set aside.

Hint: Drywall mud comes ready mixed in tubs from hardware and building supply stores. Also, matte board scraps are available from frame shops. Sometimes they will sell you nice squares cut from their scraps at a discounted price.

2. Scoop some mud you wish to color into each cup. Three colors is nice for beginning.
3. Add a little bit of coloring to each cup of mud.
4. Stir with a wooden spreading stick or spoon until mixed thoroughly. Leave at least one stick in each cup. Everyone loves watching the bright color mix with the white mud.
5. Spread colored mud onto the prepared board, mixing and blending hues, tints, and shades directly on the white board.
6. Set out of the way to dry for two or three days.

Variations

Use tools to draw designs in the colored mud, such as combs, cookie cutters, forks, spatula, or toothpicks. Color dry mud with art tissue scraps stuck on with liquid starch or thinned white glue.
Make handprints in the wet mud.

Materials

drywall mud (we will call it mud)
spreading/mixing sticks, such as tongue depressors
cardboard or matte board scraps
plastic storage cups with lids
any color source, such as food coloring or watercolor or tempera paint

Face Paint Plus

Face painting is always a big hit with adventurous artists! Now artists can paint their faces (or a friend's face), lift a print, and make a mask!

MATERIALS

heavy paper
scissors
tempera paint
    (BioColor paint
    works great)
small paintbrushes
decorations (see list)
yarn, string, or elastic
mirror

PROCESS

1. With adult help, cut heavy paper into oval shapes, about 10" (25 cm) long. To find the location of where eyeholes should be placed, hold the paper gently over an artist's face and feel where the eyes are located. Mark with wet dots from fingers dipped in water. Remove and cut the eyeholes.
2. With tempera paint or a face paint recipe (see pages 85-86), the artist paints his or her own face. It's also fun to paint a friend's face.
3. Place the oval paper over the painted face so you can see through the eyeholes. Gently rub and press to lift a print from the face onto the paper. Let paint dry.
4. Decorate the oval as a mask with feathers, sequins, yarn, and other trims.
5. Punch a hole on each side of mask. Tie strings or elastic onto the masks through the side holes. Tie it on, and look in the mirror to see the results!

DECORATIONS FOR THE MASK

beads	glue
buttons	hole punch
crinkled paper	sequins
feathers	stickers

VARIATION

Make a mural of face and handprints for the wall.

Plaster Bandage Art

Who would have guessed that plaster bandages could be used for simple, quick-drying sculptures? There's no emergency, nothing broken, just time for sculpting fun!

Process

1. Tear off a big piece of heavy-duty aluminum foil and form into a large ball or other simple bold shape. This will be the form for the plaster sculpture.
2. Cut plaster bandage into strips 3"-6" (8 cm-15cm) long. Dip a strip of bandage in the warm water and place on the foil shape. Dip bandages in the water, one after another, until the foil shape is completely covered.

Hint: Purchase fast-setting bandages on a roll from a medical supply store or from a veterinarian.

3. If you are using fine glitter dust, roll the sculpture in the glitter dust while it is still wet.

Hint: Fine glitter dust is available from rubberstamp, stationary, and most school supply stores.

4. Now let the sculpture dry. It should take about an hour.
5. If the sculpture was rolled in glitter, it need not be painted. However, if you wish to paint your sculpture, paint with any paint that is on hand! Add some glitter at the end to make it sparkly.
6. Make several sculptures and display them together.

Materials

heavy-duty aluminum foil
plaster bandage roll
scissors
warm water in a mixing bowl
fine glitter dust or regular glitter, optional
paint and paintbrushes, optional

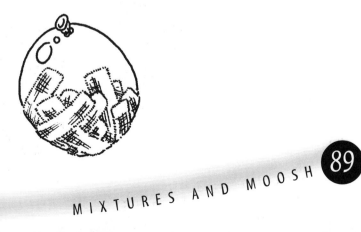

Variations

Cover a small balloon with bandages. Dry. Pop the balloon, pull it out, and paint the plaster form. Add a thread to hang. These make great party or holiday decorations.

⊙ ② 🎁 Crepe Paper Mashed Dough

Dough made from crepe paper? It's positively messy, extremely colorful, and remarkably moldable. Save those birthday party decorations for a post-birthday art party!

MATERIALS

crepe paper roll, any
    kind, any color
regular bucket
water
newspapers
old towels
rubber gloves, optional
measuring cup
small bucket or bowl
flour
salt
cardboard or bread-
    board for kneading
empty jar or can

PROCESS

1. By hand, shred one roll of any kind of crepe paper into a regular bucket and soak with water overnight.
2. The next day, drain and squeeze out the water. Place newspapers and old towels under the bucket to catch spills and soak up extra water.

Clean-up tip: Wear rubber gloves if you don't want to stain your skin.

3. Measure 1 cup (250 mL) of this packed-down paper into a small bucket or bowl. Then add 1/2 cup (125 ml) flour and 1/4 cup (60 mL) salt for each cup of paper. Make as many cupfuls as you have paper mash on hand.
4. Mix and squeeze together by hand. Use rubber gloves to keep the dye from the crepe paper off hands.
5. When well mixed, turn out on cardboard or a breadboard and knead until like dough.
6. Use this dough to mold small figures or bowls. This paper dough works especially well if molded around an old peanut butter or mayonnaise jar, or around a coffee can.
7. Allow the dough to dry on the form. Do not remove it from the form. This dough can be painted, but usually is bright enough without any additional color.

Marbled Gift Bags

Marbleized paper looks swirly and wavy like the surface design of the stone called marble, or like the designs seen in round glass marbles. This technique uses liquid starch and acrylic paints; it's quite messy and quite a bit fabulous!

PROCESS

1. Pour a very shallow layer, about 1/4" (6 mm), of liquid starch in the cookie sheet.
2. Mix the paints with a small, pointed brush in the jar lids. Mix about 3 teaspoons (15 mL) paint with 1 teaspoon (5 mL) water. The paint should be drippy and thin. Mix several colors, one per lid.
3. With the pointed brush, drip some drops of the paint on the liquid starch. Make drops here and there all over the cookie sheet. Use more than one color if you want the colors to swirl.
4. Swirl the drops together gently with a pencil or other tool. There is not much time to swirl before the paint starts sinking down into the starch.
   Hint: Try toothpicks glued to a rectangle of cardboard (see illustration).
5. Gently touch one side of a white bakery bag right on the swirled paint on top of the starch. Then gently lift the bag straight up, capturing the design as the bag is peeled off the starch.
6. Rinse the paint side of the bag in the clear water to remove the starch. Just a quick little rinse will do. Then let the marbled gift bag dry, paint side up, on newspapers.
7. Drip more paint on the starch and make more marbled gift bags.

MATERIALS

liquid starch
cookie sheet with sides
non-toxic acrylic paints in squeeze tubes
jars lids
water
teaspoons
small pointed paintbrushes or similar tools,
tools for swirling, such as a pencil or bamboo skewer
white bakery bags
sink or roasting pan filled with clear water
newspapers

Swirling tool

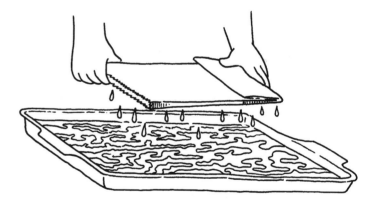

Newspaper Moosh

Tired of the same old papier-mâché? Here's an easier mooshy rendition useful for modeling-like clay or covering cardboard boxes. Be creative and incorporate magazine pictures to add a personal touch!

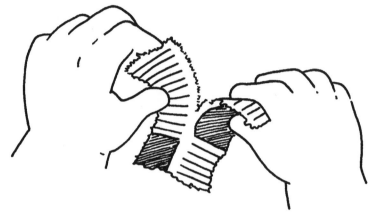

Materials

newspaper
bucket or bowl filled
   with water
old towels or rags
flour paste (see recipe)
colorful art tissue
liquid starch or
   thinned white glue
   and water
paintbrush
magazine pictures and
   photos
clear acrylic coating
   (adult only)

Flour Paste Recipe

1/2 cup (125 mL) flour
1/2 cup (125 mL) water
bowl
spoon
Mix flour and water thoroughly until smooth. Recipe can be doubled or tripled as needed.

½ CUP FLOUR   ½ CUP WATER

Newspaper Moosh (continued)

PROCESS

1. Tear newspaper into 1" (3 cm) squares. Soak in water until mooshy or pulpy.
2. Drain and squeeze out by hand. Have rags and towels on hand for drips and wet hands.
3. Next, add enough flour paste (see recipe on page 92) to make the moosh hold together.
4. Knead until workable.
5. Use as a clay to make small sculptures, or press over a form such as a small cardboard box. Dry overnight or until completely dry and hard.
6. For a personal touch, when the moosh is dry, cover it with a layer of colored art tissue, magazine pictures, or photos painted on with liquid starch or a mixture of white glue and water thinned until a consistency that will paint well.
7. Dry completely.
8. As an optional step to protect and add shine, an adult can spray the moosh art with a clear acrylic coating. Hobby and craft stores have many choices of coatings that can be sprayed or brushed on to add shine and protection.

VARIATIONS

Cover cardboard tubes to make a cylinder sculpture.
Paint sculptures instead of covering them with colorful tissue.

Blender Paper and Photo Display

One of the most beautiful art projects is homemade paper created with a blender. The best part of this activity is jumping on the paper to squeeze out the water! Use this thick artsy paper to display photographs taken by the artists.

MATERIALS

paper scraps (see list)
dishpans
water
blender
window screen, about
    12" x 20" (30 cm x 50
    cm)
newspaper, lots
camera and film,
    optional
iron, clean paper, and
    ironing board,
    optional
scissors

PROCESS

Homemade blender paper is an adult-artist cooperative project, with adult help necessary from beginning to end. The artist is the designer in this project with adult assistance at all times.

1. Tear paper scraps into small pieces. Put torn paper into dishpans and cover with water. Let soak overnight.

Hint: If working with a group, each artist can make his or her own "special pulp" in a Styrofoam cup and soak it overnight.

2. Put a handful of wet paper into the blender and cover with water. Blend until "slurry." (Slurry is a goopy wet paper pulp mash.) Scoop out the paper pulp and spread it on the window screen over a dishpan. Let water run out into the pan.

3. Meanwhile, open up a section of the daily newspaper. Place the screen on one side. Close the other side of the paper over the screen. Then flip the entire paper/screen package over, placing it on the floor.

4. Walk on the screen in socks to squeeze out some water. Try to cover the entire screen in little steps. Then jump up and down on the paper/screen package to squeeze out the rest of the water.

5. Open up the newspaper and remove the screen. Peel the paper from the screen and place it on a single sheet of newspaper to dry.

Blender Paper and Photo Display (continued)

6. While the paper is drying, if desired, take pictures with the loaded camera of scenes, friends, pets, or family that later can be mounted on the blender paper. The paper and photographs add a special touch to gifts or celebrations. Old photos that are on hand are fine too. The developing time gives the paper time to dry.

7. As an optional step for a hot-press finish, iron the paper gently. To do this, place the dry paper on some clean sheets of paper or an old clean tea towel on the ironing board. Iron gently on a medium heat.

8. Choose a photo (or anything else) to mount on the new paper. If necessary, cut the new paper into two to four smaller squares that will fit each photograph.

9. Mount the photos. Then display, place in an album, or highlight in a picture frame.

GREAT PAPER SCRAPS TO TRY

art tissue	lunch sacks
cereal boxes	magazine pictures
coloring books	maps
comics	newspaper ads
computer paper	note cards
construction paper bits	playing cards
egg cartons	post cards
envelopes	stationary
funny papers	tea boxes
gift bags	tissue
gift wrap	toilet paper
greeting cards	
junk mail	

ARTISTIC SUGGESTIONS

Blend ingredients, such as the following, into the paper pulp to add flecks and interest:

> cinnamon or turmeric
> colored sand
> colored thread
> colorful lint from the dryer
> dried flower petals
> dried tea leaves
> glitter
> gold thread
> leaf bits, grasses, weeds
> paint, food coloring, or crepe paper to color the paper
> personal materials like bits of cloth, lace, and photographs
> rosemary (fresh or dried)
> shredded ribbon
> spices
> stickers and stamps
> tiny bits of foil or metallic paper

A coarse blend of pulp lets paper particles show in the finished product.

For scented paper, add vanilla, orange, cherry, almond, or mint extracts. Adding perfume or toilet water adds scent too. Try one scent at a time.

Shredded paper and other unusual paper is often available from local printing shops for free.

To keep unused pulp for reuse, pour pulp and water from tubs through a strainer (sometimes put your hand in and swirl around to unclog the pulp). Use hands to squeeze out as much excess water as possible. Allow to dry.

Blender Paper and Photo Display (continued)

MORE PAPER EXPLORATIONS!

Crepe paper has heavy, bright dye in it. Adding little pieces of crepe paper to the finished
pulp when it's ready to set up on the screen will add streaks of color to the dry paper.

Add bits of paper from magazines with words or pictures on them to the finished pulp just
before setting up the paper to dry on the screen. The graphics and words on the torn bits
will show in the dry paper.

Funny papers and comics add color to the paper.

Press wet paper sheets to a window and they will dry that way.

VARIATIONS

Make any size pieces of paper needed for photo or other projects.

Use homemade paper to display artwork, or to make gift cards or gift tags.

Pat the wet paper pulp around the edges of picture mats to make frames.

Put colorful paper pulp in squeeze bottles (like those for picnic mustard and ketchup use)
and squeeze out designs on a matte board or other paper.

Make a paper pulp bowl by spreading strained pulp inside a bowl that is lined with plastic
wrap and sprayed with cooking spray (or rubbed with petroleum jelly). It's like lining a pie
pan with pastry dough! Dry completely. Paint with clear hobby acrylic to seal. Do not use
the bowl for anything other than decoration as moisture will soften and ruin it.

Chapter 5
Adventurous Ideas

Toilet Paper Play Day

Children love toilet paper! Wrapping each other with long streamers of toilet paper is great fun and makes for a play day sculpture that will not be forgotten.

MATERIALS

rolls of toilet paper
2 or more artists

PROCESS

1. Begin by unwrapping or unrolling a roll of toilet paper a bit. See how it works. Don't be surprised to see the roll of paper bouncing across the floor as it unravels.
2. For the first play sculpture, one person volunteers to be the sculpture model, and the other volunteers to be the artist. The artist wraps the sculpture model with toilet paper in anyway enjoyable to both. Make an entire mummy, or try other costumes or designs.
3. When one sculpture is finished, trade places!
4. Use leftover sculpture paper for making homemade paper (page 94) or paper dough (page 92).

VARIATIONS

Make outfits for toy animals or dolls.
Make a huge pile of toilet paper to hide in.
Wrap furniture like the famous artist, Cristo.
Wrap objects in toilet paper to disguise them.
Stack rolls of toilet paper like blocks.
Cover a doorway with strips of toilet paper.
Create a spider web or maze with toilet paper in an entire room.
Use toilet paper to create a hiding house, cloud world, or other pretend area.
Paint with a roll of toilet paper.
Drip paint, food coloring, or paper dyes on a roll of toilet paper.

Exuberant Tube Garland

This draping garland can decorate all four walls of an entire room, suitable for any happy occasion, or simply to use up all those tubes saved from wrapping paper, paper towels, and toilet paper.

PROCESS

1. Save about 100 paper towel tubes and other cardboard tubes.
2. Decorate each tube. Some suggestions are:
   - Paint the tubes with tempera paints, and dry.
   - Place art tissue over the tubes with thinned white glue or liquid starch, and dry.
   - Tape construction paper scraps on the tubes, or wrap the tubes in construction paper.
   - Paste wrapping paper over the tubes.
   - Cover the tubes with stickers, labels, or other stick-on decorations.
   - Draw on the labels or scraps with markers.
3. Cut the drinking straws into sections.
4. String the tubes on heavy string, placing a small paper plate, a drinking straw, and another paper plate between each tube in a repeating pattern. This will form a garland with spaces between the tubes and will help keep the tubes separated.

Hint: Use the points of the scissors to poke holes in the cupcake papers or the paper plates.

5. Measure the garland now and then to see if it will reach around the entire room. Keep adding tubes and other garland materials until the garland is long enough. You may need to add extra string.
6. Drape the garland around the room from sturdy points such as door casings and window casings. The garland will be heavy.

MATERIALS

cardboard tubes from paper towels, wrapping paper, or toilet paper
materials to decorate tubes (see step # 2)
plastic drinking straws
scissors
heavy string or twine
cupcake papers or small paper plates

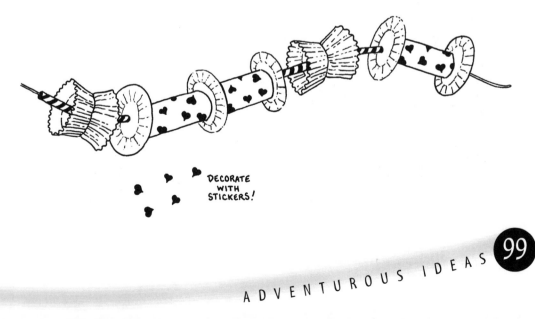

DECORATE WITH STICKERS!

Play Pasta Primavera

Make artful imaginary spaghetti with string pasta and red paint sauce. *Get ready for an artistic cooking jumble!*

Materials

string
scissors
big, old cooking pot
big bowl
red tempera paint
white glue
measuring cup
mixing brush or stick
tongs
cardboard or card-
    board pizza circle
glitter in a shaker,
    optional
construction paper,
    optional

Process

1. Cut string (imaginary spaghetti) into 12"-18" (30 cm-40 cm) lengths.
2. Fill the old cooking pot with string pieces.
3. Fill the bowl with red paint (imaginary sauce) 1"-2" (3 cm-5 cm) deep. Mix in 1/4 cup (60 mL) white glue. Stir until mixed.
3. Grab a bunch of "spaghetti" with the tongs. Dip into the "red sauce." Arrange on the cardboard. Sprinkle with glitter "cheese."
4. If desired, add other ingredients to the silly spaghetti, such as construction paper cutouts of olives, mushrooms, or sausage. They will stick to the red glue "sauce" without additional glue.

Variations

Make green pesto sauce paint or yellow cheese sauce paint.
Chop crinkled paper into little pieces to resemble Parmesan cheese.
Make string paintings by dragging, daubing, and dipping strings covered in paint across any paper.

Fly Swatter Painting

Whap! Splat! Smack! *Fly swatters make the most enjoyable noises and prints when they are dipped in paint and then smacked against the paper! This activity is always a hit. Fair warning: watch for flying paint specks and splatters!*

PROCESS

1. Unroll butcher or craft paper on a table, floor, or the lawn. Tape corners down, or weight with rocks.
2. Pour paint into shallow containers.
3. Place the pans of paint around the edges of the paper with a fly swatter in each pan.
4. Press the fly swatter in the paint, gently lift out, and slap against the paper to make prints. Keep swatting until the prints begin to fade, then re-dip and make more prints.

Hint: Most of the paint that flips off the fly swatter occurs when first lifted from the paper. It tends to stick a bit and then let go, flipping paint when it releases. Artists also tend to want to slap the swatters in the paint pans like they do on the paper, and may need reminding to only press or dip the swatters in paint, and slap away freely on the paper.

5. When the paper is filled with fly swatter designs and prints, let it dry where it is, or move the paper to a drying area, roll out more paper, and start again!
6. When done, rinse the fly swatters and pans for another day.

VARIATIONS

Slap a fly swatter onto a table covered with shaving cream and see what happens! Stand back! You may need to wear goggles or sunglasses!

MATERIALS

butcher paper or craft paper
tape or rocks
tempera paint
shallow containers
clean fly swatters

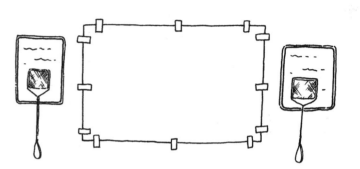

SMACK!

Ocu-less Painting

What is painting like when you can't see what you're painting? No matter the outcome, the process is fun and extraordinary every time!

MATERIALS

blindfold (a bandana works great)
paper
paint easel or paper taped to a wall
paint
paintbrushes

PROCESS

1. Gently tie a blindfold over the artist's eyes. Lead the artist to the paint easel.
2. Stand the artist in front of a paint easel, which has been prepared with paper, paints, and brushes and is ready to go. No peaking allowed!

Hint: It's fun to ask the artist beforehand what colors to put out, but don't let him or her see!

3. The artist feels the paper, the cups of paint, the location of brushes, and then begins painting!
4. The artist paints until satisfied that the artwork is complete. Then remove the blindfold.
5. What a surprise!
6. Try another painting on a fresh sheet of paper. Do the results change?

VARIATIONS

Try other types of artwork while blindfolded, such as

clay or playdough	cut-and-paste collage
drawing or coloring	fingerpainting
watercolor painting	wood scrap sculpture

Try other games or activities while blindfolded, such as

"watching" TV	hearing a story
putting together puzzles	walking (with guidance)

Charcoal Drawing

Charcoal offers a good space for little (or big) artists to experiment with drawing, shading, and smearing while working on an extra big piece of paper taped to the wall.

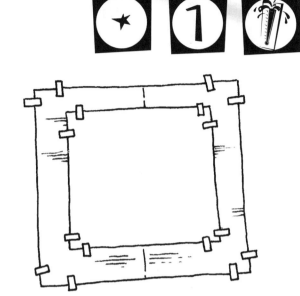

PROCESS

1. First tape newspaper to the wall to cover a slightly bigger area than the art paper will cover. Then tape the art paper in the middle of the newspaper. The newspaper protects the wall around the outside edge of the paper.
2. Draw on the large paper with charcoal sticks.

Clean-up tip: Charcoal is very messy. Have a damp towel on hand to wipe fingers now and then if desired. Charcoal drawings store well if first rolled into a tube and secured with a rubber band.

3. Explore the blending and smearing characteristics of charcoal with bare hands, fingers, or other tools like tissues and cotton balls.
4. Remove from the wall or leave on display.
5. Wash up with soap and water, but dry with old towels!

VARIATIONS

Place the paper on a textured wall or sidewalk to pick up the bumps under the paper with the charcoal.

Make rubbings of anything, inside or out. Many people enjoy making rubbings of words and pictures on buildings, signs, tombstones, or plaques.

Offer several widths and sizes of charcoal.

MATERIALS

newspaper
tape
big sheet of paper, such as craft paper or butcher paper
artist's charcoal
damp towel
tissues, cotton balls, sponges, cotton swabs

COTTON SWABS, SPONGES, RAGS AND COTTON BALLS

Pow! Paint

If you like messy and thrilling rolled into one exciting art project, this is it! Put the ingredients into a baggie, stand back, and POW! An explosive piece of art!

MATERIALS

large piece of paper
paper towels
scissors
baking soda
measuring cups and
    spoons
thin, bright paint of
    any kind
white vinegar
zipper-closure plastic
    baggies

PROCESS

1. Spread out a large sheet of plain paper on the ground outside or in a nice big space inside.
2. Prepare the paint bags. Start by cutting a paper towel into fourths.
3. Put 2 tablespoons (30 mL) baking soda into the middle of a paper towel square.
4. To make a paper towel pillow to hold the baking soda, fold over the sides and then the ends of the paper towel around the pile of baking soda. Place the pillow of baking soda into a baggie.
5. Add 2 teaspoons (10 mL) paint to 1 cup (250 mL) white vinegar. Pour the colored vinegar into the baggie with the baking soda pillow. Quickly close the baggie and place it on the big piece of paper. Stand back! The baking soda and vinegar will mix and pop the bag open to explode paint onto the paper.
6. Do many explosions for one painting or one explosion per painting.

VARIATIONS

Experiment with different types of paint or food coloring.
Use cardboard or extra heavy paper, bigger bags, and/or more ingredients.

DROP INTO BAG....

QUICKLY CLOSE THE BAG AND PLACE IT ON YOUR PAPER. STAND BACK!

Centenary Box Mobile

One hundred days of the year, 100 years old, 100 days of rain! Celebrate by collecting "100's" of items to help create a hanging centenary box. This activity is fine for an individual, and hundreds times bigger and more fun for a group.

PROCESS

This project is written for a group of artists working together; however, an individual artist could easily do the same project by saving several collections of 100 items.

1. A plain cardboard mailing box without words is best. If desired, wrap the box with plain paper after step #4.
2. Poke a hole in one corner of the box. Tie a very large knot on one end of the string. Poke the string from the inside of the box out through the hole, so the knot remains inside the box and the rest of the string is outside.
3. Tape the knot to the inside of the box for extra strength. Use as much tape as you think you need to make the string hold the box well for hanging.
4. Glue and tape the box closed.
5. Each child brings a collection of 100 collage items to the work area.
6. The group decides how and where the collections will be glued to the box.

Hint: Some artists will want to group them, others will want to spread them out, and still others will want to make borders and designs. Sometimes group members will each choose a part of the box that becomes individual space. Some groups like to draw the designs with markers or crayons first.

7. The group glues on the collections of 100 to the box in whatever way they have decided to proceed.

MATERIALS

cardboard box, in a large cube shape
plain paper and tape, optional
scissors
heavy duty string or fish line
tape
glue
collection of hundreds of items (see list on page 106)
markers, crayons

POKE A HOLE

LARGE KNOT

TAPE THE KNOT SECURELY INSIDE THE BOX.

8. Allow the collections to dry briefly.
9. Hang the box from the ceiling from the string at the corner. Watch it spin and move, displaying hundreds and hundreds of special collections of 100. Use to help celebrate 100 of anything, or marvel at what 100 looks like over and over again. (Ten collections of 100 make 1000. That's something to think about!)

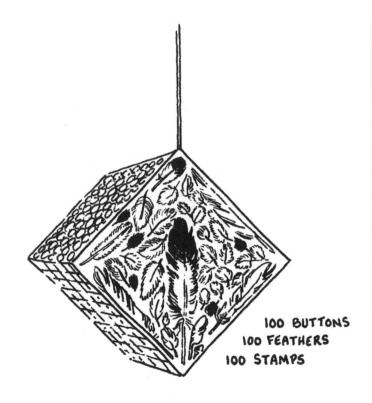

100 BUTTONS
100 FEATHERS
100 STAMPS

THINGS TO CONSIDER COLLECTING

beads
bread bag tags
buttons
computer chips
cotton balls
craft sticks
feathers
googly eyes
labels
mini-marshmallows
pebbles
scraps of paper
small sticks
tea bags

VARIATIONS

Hang the box before gluing the collections in place to develop cooperative skills while gluing and holding a hanging, moving box.

Cover the box with paper before adding collections. Wrapping paper is a festive and fun choice as a background.

Hang 10 small boxes on strings from a stick. Glue one collection of 100 to each small box.

Stop, Drop, and Paint

Do you know anyone who isn't fascinated by bubble wrap? But would they volunteer to be wrapped in it? This project makes comical bubbly prints, if everyone can stop laughing long enough to try it!

PROCESS

1. First, with adult help, construct the bubble printing chamber. Cut off the top and bottom of the appliance box. Cut a door on one side that can be closed after the bubble-wrapped artist enters.
2. Cover the inside of the box with large sheets of craft paper. Attach with tape.
3. Open the door for the artist to enter when ready, after step 6.
4. Wrap a volunteer artist in bubble wrap. Make tubes around the legs, arms, the entire body (but not the head, face, or feet). Make sure the artist can still walk. Wrap as much or as little as the artist would enjoy.

Clean-up tip: The artist should wear old clothing or even an old raincoat or garbage bag to protect clothing.

5. Fill shallow pie pans with tempera paint to about 1/4"-1/2" deep (6 mm-13 mm).

Clean-up tip: Mix tempera paints with baby shampoo to make clean-up easier.

6. Take paint rollers and roll in the paint. Then roll the paint onto the bubble wrap. Use as many colors as you wish.
7. Now the bubble-wrapped and painted artist enters the paint chamber. Close the door but peek over the top to watch. The artist turns around and gently but firmly bumps into the walls making bubble wrap prints on the craft paper. When done, unwrap the artist (but save the bubble wrap for the next time), take the paper off the inside of the box, and remove it from the box. Set up another for the next volunteer!

MATERIALS

cardboard appliance box
scissors or sharp knife (adult only)
big craft paper
tape
all sorts of bubble wrap
tempera paint
shallow pans
paint rollers

REFRIGERATOR

← INSIDE OF CARTON LINED WITH PAPER.

VARIATIONS

Simplified version: Make bubble wrap prints by rolling on paper taped to the floor or wall.

Wrap objects in bubble wrap to make prints, such as a playground ball, a rolling pin, or a cardboard box.

Cover the sole of a shoe with bubble wrap or make bubble-wrap mittens for making prints.

Staple things to an old raincoat. Put on the raincoat, paint the coat, and then make prints.

Paint a Ball

Dangle a ball *from the ceiling and then try to paint it. Need an additional challenge? Use only one hand.*

Process

1. First, tie a long enough piece of string to the ball (beach balls or punch balls both have perfect places to tie a string) so that it can hang from the ceiling at the artist's eye level.
2. To cover the ball in paper before painting, make a big cylinder-tube with the paper by wrapping it around the ball. Then tape to hold. (See illustration). Gather the top of the paper tube and tape it down, keeping the string free. Do the same for the bottom of the tube. Press down any pleats and wrinkles, but don't worry about them; they will add to the painted design.
3. Tape, tie, or staple the string to the ceiling.
4. To begin, dip a brush in paint and try to paint the ball using one hand. Do not steady the ball with the other hand.
5. Let the painting dry on the ball. Leave the painting on the ball as a display, or remove the paper from the ball, carefully undoing the gathering of the paper (see how the pleats and gathers enhanced the paint design). Let dry on a flat surface.

Variation

Make a dodecahedron out of paper for a ball painting that can be saved.(A dodecahedron is made from ten circles stapled together at the edges to create a globe shape. See the illustration.)

Materials
string
scissors
ball
large piece of paper
tape and stapler
tempera paints
paintbrushes

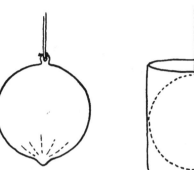
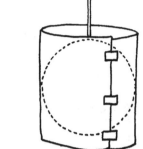

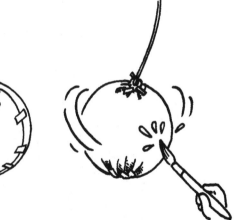
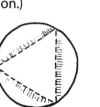

Big, Big Box Puzzle

Constructing a puzzle *is a visually absorbing activity, but designing one that has six sides per puzzle-piece is completely captivating! Nine tall tissue boxes supply the beginning of a challenging and creative puzzle that is Big, Bigger, and Biggest!*

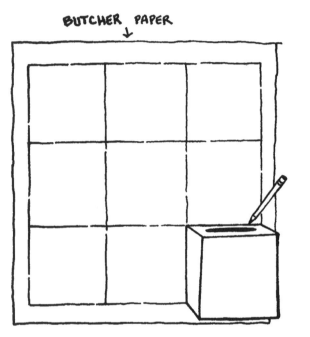

BUTCHER PAPER

Materials

9 empty tissue boxes, tall style
pencil
big sheet of white butcher paper or craft paper
markers, crayons, pens, pencils
scissors
glue, tape

Process

Little Puzzle (1-sided, 9 boxes)

1. With a pencil, trace one tissue box on its biggest side (not the top or bottom) on the butcher paper. Make nine joined tracings, three across and three down, edges touching, that will form one square with nine sections. Set the box aside. (See illustration.)
2. Draw one whole picture on the nine-sectioned square that fills or covers all nine sections. Color it brightly and boldly.
3. Cut apart all nine sections of the picture. Glue or tape each part of the drawing on one side of each tissue box (not the top or bottom, sides only).
4. Now scoot all the boxes together to match the original picture. It's a nine-piece puzzle!

Big, Big Box Puzzle (continued)

Big, Big Puzzle (6-sided, 9 boxes)
Process

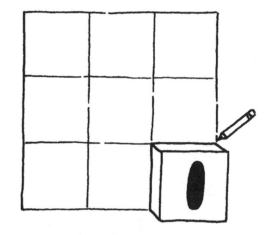

Each side of the tissue box will be part of one of six puzzles, with each puzzle having nine sections.

1. Repeating the same method as above, make another complete puzzle picture. Again, the picture puzzle will have nine parts, three across and three down, just as before.

Hint: Pictures can be real things, scenes, or wild and crazy abstract drawings, or cut up an old poster or print, or cut out magazine pictures or wrapping papers instead of drawing or coloring.

2. Cut apart the squares and glue each one to each box, one on each big side of a tissue box.

3. Repeat the picture puzzle method, making two more complete pictures, and gluing them on the set of nine boxes. Each box will have two remaining empty sides, the tops and bottoms. That means two more puzzle pictures to do!

4. Trace the top of the box nine times, three across and three down. This will form a smaller square than before, but will still have nine sections. Make a picture on this square. Cut them apart just like before, and glue them all, each to one box top.

5. Repeat the above step, making nine more squares for the remaining bottom part of the tissue box. Make a picture on this square, then cut this picture apart and glue or tape it to the remaining empty bottom of each box.

6. Now the tissue boxes are completely covered on each side with a picture puzzle.

7. Can you make all six different puzzles match, one at a time, rolling the boxes over and over, moving them about, until a puzzle picture is complete?

Memory Quilt

Create a quilt *that will be an artistic heirloom for the lucky recipient. Don't be surprised if everyone decides they want one of these memorable quilts for their very own!*

MATERIALS

white sheet or fabric
fabric crayons
measuring tape
old scissors
sandpaper
electric warming tray
work gloves or hot
    mitts, optional
old iron and ironing
    board
paper for the ironing
    step
quilted fabric for back
    of quilt, any pattern
sewing machine,
    sewing needs like
    thread and pins
yarn and a heavy
    needle

SANDPAPER

PROCESS

Making this quilt involves both heat and electricity and requires constant adult interaction, assistance, and supervision.

1. Use a measuring tape and fabric crayons to mark 8" (20 cm) squares on the sheet. Set aside.
2. Cut sandpaper into 8" (20 cm) squares with old scissors. Make one sandpaper square for each square on the sheet.
3. Place a sandpaper square on the heated warming tray, sand side up.

Hint: Use caution and supervision when working around a heat source, although the electric warming tray should be safe to touch briefly. Wear work gloves or hot mitts from the kitchen on the non-drawing hand, if desired.

4. The artist carefully colors a design or picture on the sandpaper, watching the crayon markings melt into the rough sand. Set aside and let cool. Make one sandpaper square for each square of the sheet.
5. To transfer the crayon squares to the fabric, heat the old iron to cotton setting. Spread clean paper on the ironing board.
6. Place the sandpaper drawing face down on one of the marked off squares on the sheet (sandy picture side against the cloth, sandpaper backing facing up). Cover all with a clean piece of paper to protect the iron. Then press the back of the sandpaper to transfer the picture to the cloth. Press firmly. Do not wiggle the iron too much.

Memory Quilt (continued)

7. An adult constructs the quilt with as much help from the artist (or artists) as is appropriate. When all the squares have been ironed onto the sheet, cut a piece of the quilt backing to the size of the sheet. Choose a fabric that is already quilted, has a nice pattern, and is soft and cuddly. Turn both fabrics inside out (good sides facing each other), matching edges and corners, and sew three sides together with straight stitches on the sewing machine. Sew the fourth side almost closed, leaving about 10" (25 cm) open. Turn them right-side out and sew the remainder of the fourth side closed. Iron the seams flat. To hold the layers of fabric together, at the corner of each quilted square, sew a piece of yarn through both layers of fabric and back to the front, and then tie tightly in a little knot.
8. The quilt is ready to be given as a gift, or enjoyed as a wall hanging, throw, or naptime friend.

Variations

Make wall decorations or pillows out of individual squares.
Use this melting and ironing process to decorate T-shirts or other articles of clothing.
Create a tablecloth or table runner instead of a quilt.

SANDPAPER IS DESIGN SIDE DOWN, SANDWICHED BETWEEN CLOTH AND PAPER....

Days on End Weaving

This is one of those phenomenal activities that can span several age groups and go on and on for days, growing and building in design and character. When the weaving is finished, display this beautiful, cooperative weaving for all to enjoy.

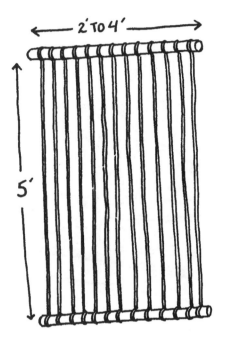

MATERIALS

2 wooden dowels 2'- 4' (60 cm-120 cm) long
heavy string
scissors
table
2 heavy, fairly thick boards (about 3'-4' long) (1 m-2 m)
duct tape
weaving materials (see list on next page)

MAKE THE LOOM
PROCESS

1. Cut the heavy string into 5' (1.5 m) lengths. Make twenty to thirty pieces.
2. Tie the end of each string to one dowel, spacing them about 2" (5 cm) apart.
3. Tie the other ends of each string to the second dowel, again about 2" (5 cm) apart. Both dowels should hang parallel to each other and the strings should be taut and even. Some adjustment may be necessary to make all the strings tight.

SET UP THE LOOM

1. Construct a set-up for the loom on the table to raise it off the table and make weaving easy for little hands. To begin, place a thick heavy board at each end of the table. Then stretch the dowels and strings over a table from one board to the other.
2. When they are lined up, tuck one dowel around one heavy board.
3. Tape the board to the table.
4. Pull the other dowel and strings very tight to the other board, roll the dowel around the board, pull the board very tight so the strings are tight, and duct tape that board to the table. Be sure the strings are pulled as tight as you can.

Days on End Weaving (continued)

BEGIN WEAVING

1. Weave (over under, over under) with ribbons and other materials through the strings beginning at the top and continuing down.
2. Slip each line of weaving up close to the prior line or leave it loose for design purposes. Have fun with the selection of materials for the weaving. Explore patterns for weaving, like "over two, under three" or "over one, under five."
3. Leave the weaving up so artists can work on it for several days, or as long as it takes to weave it all the way to the bottom.
4. When the weaving is complete, cut and peel away the tape. Hang the weaving on the wall to enjoy.

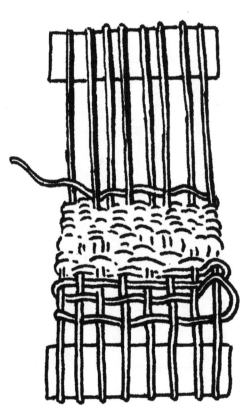

WEAVING MATERIALS TO TRY

crepe paper
jute
long thin leaves
plastic surveyor's tape
ribbons (gift, curling, or fabric types)

rope
sewing trims
torn strips of fabric
twine
yarn

VARIATIONS

Instead of using dowels and string, weave through netting such as that used for volley ball, tennis, fishing, or orange construction site netting.
Paint long strips of paper or ribbon for use in weaving.

Realistic House Sculpture

Constructing a full-size cardboard house is like building a playhouse. In fact, build it strong enough, and it is a playhouse!

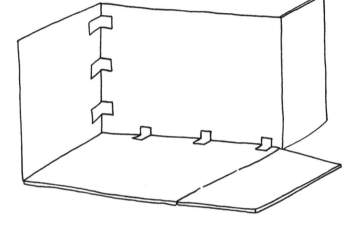

MATERIALS

cardboard appliance box(es) or large sheets of plain cardboard

sharp knife (adult only)

wide tape

materials and props to decorate the house (see list)

boxes for furniture and props (see list on page 117)

chalk, glue, glue gun (adult only), markers, scissors, stapler, tape, as needed

PROCESS

Building a realistic cardboard house requires adult interaction, supervision, and assistance throughout the cutting and assembling steps, in particular, and throughout the entire project. The artist directs the steps requiring caution.

1. Cut and unfold an appliance box to form the corner of a room. (See illustration.) Use ample tape to hold the cardboard in place. If using sheets of cardboard, tape together to form the corner of a room.

Hint: Plain cardboard sheets are usually available from office and paper supply stores.

2. Add another piece of cardboard for the floor and tape to the other two walls.

3. Decide what kind of a room this sculpture will be, such as a kitchen, bedroom, office, space ship, fairy's hideaway, vet's office, and so on. See suggestions listed on page 117. (A bedroom will be described in this write-up, but any type of room construction imaginable is possible.)

4. Prepare the walls. Glue on wallpaper, wrapping paper, fabric, or paint the walls. Next add details to the wall such as a window or door (which an adult cuts out with a sharp knife), hanging pictures, and so on. Cardboard shelves could be made from other boxes and taped to the wall. Perhaps some curtains could hang over a window.

Realistic House Sculpture (continued)

5. Create furniture from other cardboard boxes. Cut, bend, and assemble a bed, chair, dresser, and so on. Add a real pillow and blanket to the bed. Bookshelves could be built from boxes. Add real books or make some from cardboard.
6. A floor covering could be drawn on the cardboard with markers to look like wood. Add a throw rug or carpet scraps.
7. Build the room until it feels complete. Enjoy as a sculpture or, if strong enough, a room to play inside.

Suggestions of Materials and Props to Decorate the House

artwork	picture frames
blankets	pillows
cafe curtains	plastic plants
carpet scraps	throw rug
clear plastic wrap (for windows)	toys
fabric	wallpaper
paints and brushes	wood scraps
paper	wrapping paper

Try Boxes from the Following for Furniture and Props

canned food	tissues
computers	wine
stereos	

More Suggestions of Spaces to Build

alien's world
art studio
baby nursery
bank
beach
birthday party
camp-out
cave
doctor's office
fairy's glen
hospital
kitchen
library
restaurant
Santa's workshop
school
space ship
tea-time room
Three Bear's house
tree house
undersea grotto
vet's office
zoo

Dino Sculpture

A dino-mite dino-sized sculpture! Gather some boxes, containers, and other cardboard items to form the dino shape. Cover it with chicken wire and drape in colored cheesecloth.

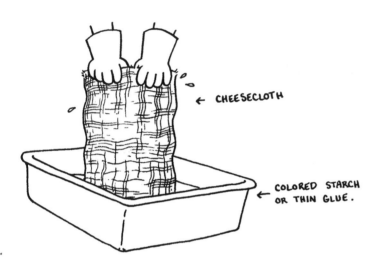

← CHEESECLOTH

← COLORED STARCH OR THIN GLUE.

MATERIALS

cardboard boxes, containers, pieces, or tubes
glue, masking tape, stapler
chicken wire
wire cutters, pliers, twist ties
dishpans
liquid starch or thinned white glue
Liquid Watercolor paints or liquid fabric coloring
cheesecloth
rubber gloves or latex gloves

PROCESS

This industrious project is an adult and artist cooperative art experience. The adult and artist should work together from beginning to end with constant adult supervision, assistance, and cooperation with the artist.

1. Stack, glue, tape, and staple various cardboard pieces together to create the basic structure of the dinosaur shape, or any other sculpture.

Hint: Some artists like to make a "real thing," while other artists like to make an abstract "something." Enjoy either!

2. Next, with adult help, use wire cutters, pliers, and twist ties to cover the cardboard with the chicken wire to make the "exoskeleton" of the dinosaur or sculpture. This is the most industrious part of the art project and may take more than one day to finish.

Hint: Make sure all sharp edges and twist tie ends are pushed toward the inside of the dino. You may want to put masking tape over the sharp wire ends.

3. To cover the sculpture form, start by filling the bottom of each dishpan with about 2" (5 cm) liquid starch or thinned white glue. Add paint or fabric dye to the pan to create the desired color.

Dino Sculpture (continued)

4. Immerse large sheets of cheesecloth, about 2' (60 cm) long, in the colored starch or thin glue. Then drape the colored cloth over the form. Repeat the draping process until the sculpture is completely covered in colored cheesecloth. Let dry at least overnight.
Hint: Wear rubber gloves to protect hands.
5. Glue on additional details and design features (eyes, claws, teeth) cut from cardboard and glue. Dry again.

Variations

Cover the form with any favorite papier-mâché recipe instead of cheesecloth. Paint when dry.
For a very abstract sculpture, skip the chicken wire step and work directly on the box form.

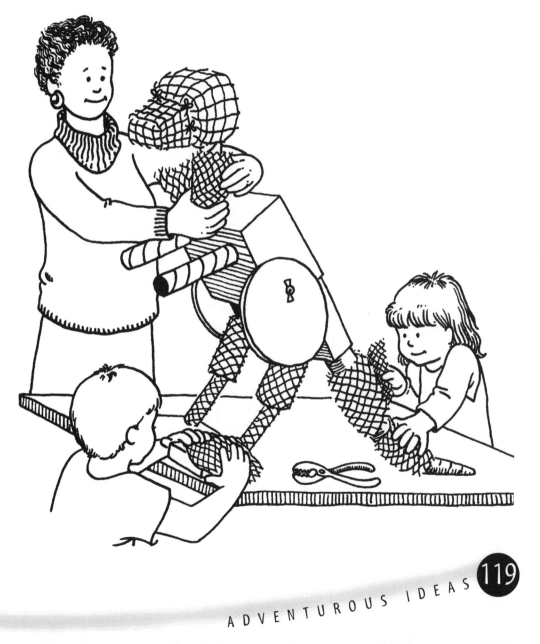

✪ ③ 🌡 ❗ Concrete Stepping Stones

Gardens large or small can be enhanced and beautified with hand-made stepping stones that are unique and personalized by the artist. Make one, make many, and tiptoe through the tulips!

FILL WITH CONCRETE ↓

← CLEAR PLASTIC POT SAUCER

SMOOTH WITH TROWEL

MATERIALS

dust mask
safety glasses
rubber work gloves
work clothing
outdoor work area
Portland cement mix
water
bucket or buckets for mixing
small trowels
mold to make the stepping stone (see list on page 121)
materials to imbed in the cement (see list on page 121)
hose and water for cleanup

PROCESS

This is an adult and child cooperative project from beginning to end. Adult help will be needed throughout the entire project, and especially in handling the concrete mix. Dress with dust masks, safety glasses, rubber gloves, and appropriate work clothing. This is messy!

1. Mix the concrete mix and water in small amounts in the bucket(s) to a consistency of thick pudding. The artist can stir and mix with a trowel. Dust masks are required for this step due to the powdery cement dust.

Hints: Someone with a strong back should lift the heavy bags of cement. Rinse buckets and trowels outside immediately after using.

2. Place the mold on a flat surface. Fill it with wet cement. Tap the sides of the mold all around several times to release any air bubbles that might weaken the stone. Smooth the top with the trowel.

Hint: If using pizza boxes, fill to about 1" (3 cm) and prop the sides with bricks for support.

3. To create a unique and personalized stepping stone, press selected objects into the wet surface. Except for leaves and flowers, press any objects in securely that are to remain in the concrete or the objects may work loose and fall out over time.

Hints about leaves and flowers: press in deeply enough to make a distinct impression; remove as the concrete sets up or leave until completely dry. (Nature will remove them over time or they can be brushed out with a sturdy brush.)

Concrete Stepping Stones (continued)

4. Let the concrete harden until firm, but it does not need to be dry. Remove the firm concrete from the mold. Then let dry several days before actually stepping on the stone.
5. Clean up with a hose and water.
6. Enjoy the stepping stones in a garden, yard, or anywhere outdoors that needs a bright spot.

MOLDS TO MAKE THE STEPPING STONES

clear plastic pot saucers (available in many sizes from garden stores)
fancy purchased molds
pizza boxes

MATERIALS TO IMBED IN THE CEMENT

aquarium rocks
beads
buttons
flowers
leaves
pebbles
rocks

BIRD'S EYE VIEW

VARIATIONS

Flowers make pretty impressions in the cement. If a flower has a large number of petals, simply pull off a few and arrange in radial pattern of your own.
Words and objects can be made with aquarium gravel, pebbles, or buttons.
Experiment with different sizes and kinds of molds.
Concrete is inexpensive, so don't worry about making mistakes.

BIG MESSY ART

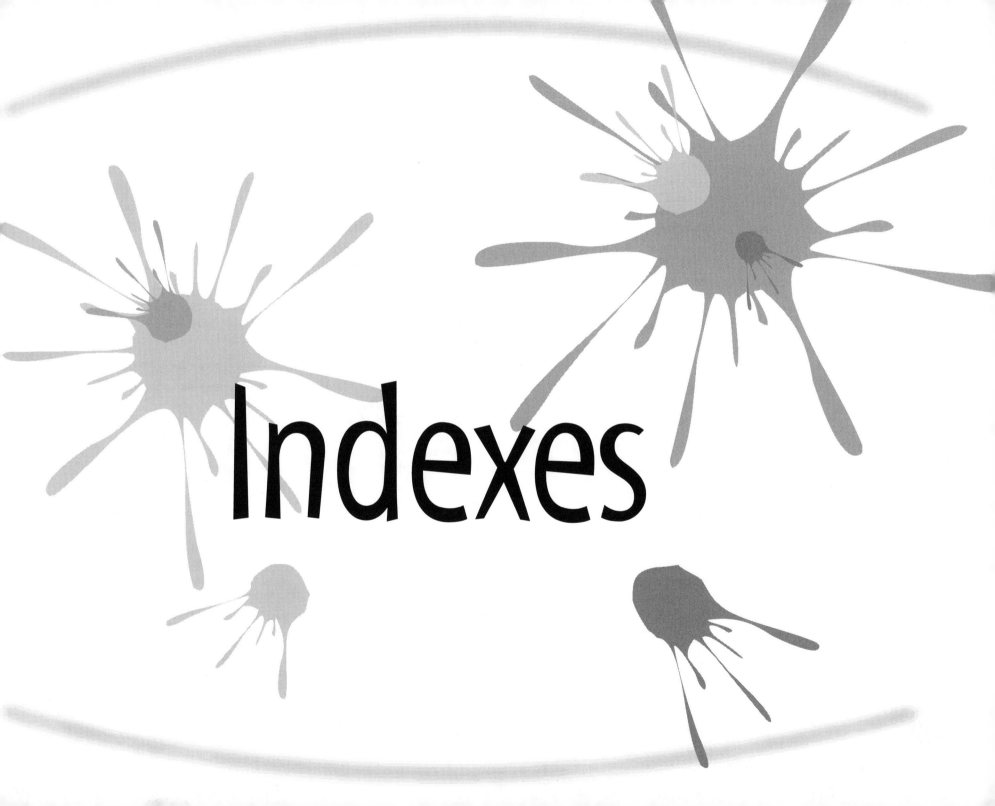

Indexes

Materials Index

A

acrylic paint, squeeze, 91
appliance box, 116
aquarium rocks, 19, 121
art gallery, 51
art tissue, 49, 87, 92-93
artist's charcoal, 103
Astroturf, 37

B

baby lotion, 85
baby's ball, 26
back massager
    wooden, 54
bag
    bakery, white, 91
    grocery, extra heavy, 104
    zipper-closure, 104
baking cups, 99
baking soda, 104
balls, 109
    baby, 26
    cat, 26
    dog, 26
    golf, 26
    lightweight, 24
    Nerf, 26
    Ping-Pong, 24
    playground, 26, 108
    rubber, 26
    softball, 26
    tennis, 17, 26
    whiffle, 26

balloons, 25
    water, small, 27
bamboo skewer, 91
bandana, 102
basket, plastic berry, 22
bath towels, white, 32
beads, 88, 106, 121
    heavy, 69
    strings of, 16
bed linen, 46, 112
bench, 29
berry basket, 22
bike, 14, 66
BioColor paint, 88
biodegradable packing peanuts, 81
blender, 94
blindfold, 102
blocks, 14
blow dryer, 24
boards, 114
    large, 51
    scraps, 51
Borax, 79
bottle, spray, 23, 32, 82
bowl
    plastic, for hat form, 81
box
    appliance, cardboard, 107, 116
    cardboard, cube, 105
    cardboard, 44, 116, 118
    cereal, 44
    lightweight, colorful, 44
    pizza, 48, 120, 121
branch, from tree, 80
bread bag tags, 106
breadboard, 90
broom, 60
broom, brush, 58
brush, 49

for glue, 40
for mixing, 100
house-painting, 51
make-up, 85
paste, 57
sponge, 66
wallpaper smoothing, 57
brushes, items other than brushes for
    painting, list, 55-56
brush-type tools, 60
bubble
    solution, 84
    solution, commercial, 22
    solution, recipe, 22
    tools, 22
    wand, 22
bubble wrap, 107
butcher paper, 14, 19-21, 24-25, 27, 31,
    36, 41, 60, 62, 64, 66, 68, 101, 103
    White, 58, 110
    See craft paper.
buttons, 16, 69, 88, 106, 121

C

camera, 94
can, 90
candy mold, 79
cardboard, 17, 39, 48-49, 61, 77, 81, 87,
    90, 104
    appliance box, cardboard, 107, 116
    box, 44, 105, 118
    box, cube, 105
    box, cereal, 44
    box, pizza, 48, 120, 121
    box, 44, 116, 118
    circle, pizza, 100
    containers, 118

lightweight, 75
lightweight, colorful, 44
little scraps, 51, 118
sheets, 30, 44, 116
sturdy, 21, 43
tube: from paper towel, toilet paper,
    wrapping paper, 93, 99, 118
carpet sample, 37
caster cups, 57
cat ball, 26
cement mix, 120
ceramic tile, 44
cereal box, 44
chain, jewelry, 16
chair, 21
chalk, 34, 48, 116
    sidewalk, large, 14
charcoal, 103
cheesecloth, 118
chicken wire, 118
child drawn pictures, 111
Christmas decorations, 50
Christmas tree lot, 58
clay, 45, 77, 102
clear acrylic coating (adult only), 92-93,
    96
clear plastic wrap, 50
cloth, bits, 95
coat hanger, 22
coating
    clear acrylic (adult only), 92, 96
    hobby, 93
cocoa, 86
coffee grounds, 74, 84
colander, 22
cold cream, 84, 86
collage items, 48, 88

Icon Index

Artist Experience Level

1—for beginning artists with little art experience

2—for artists with some art experience

3—for artists with more experience

Preparation and Planning

① 1—for projects that use easy-to-find materials and have a quick and easy set-up

② 2—for projects that use familiar materials and have a moderate set-up

③ 3—for projects that use unusual materials and have an involved set-up

Level of Messiness

1—for projects that are a little bit messy

2—for projects that are somewhat messy

3—for projects that are very messy

Caution for projects that use sharp utensils, a heat source, or any other potentially dangerous materials

Project List, alphabetical

Thanks!

Thanks you to all the adventurous parents and educators who are devoted to exploring new art ideas with children of all ages. You bring them the joy of creativity, the delight of imagination, and the thrill of adventure in art. The ideas you contributed through our e-mail sharing groups have added a dazzling assortment of extraordinary experiences to this book. My deepest thanks to each of you for your child-tested, creativity-proven contributions.

Ann Weaver, North Carolina

Ann Scalley, Massachusetts

Beth Lastovica, Texas

Betty Bowen, Oklahoma

Cheryl Joyce, New York

Chris Hancock, Texas

Dana Bowman, California

Dolores Rogish, Ohio

Dorothy (Dot) Blomstrom, Ohio

Gail Hariton, New York

Gregory Uba, California

Heather Martin, Georgia

Judi Woodards, Ohio

Karen E. Korteling, Illinois

LaDonna Dixon, South Carolina

Lauramarie Lauricella, New York

Marcie Fraade, New York

Nancy Yost, Pennsylvania

Sharon Henneborn, New Jersey

Sheila Tompkins-Hess, Nevada

Stacey Bernstein, Colorado

Yvonne Stehle, Mississippi

Recommended Titles

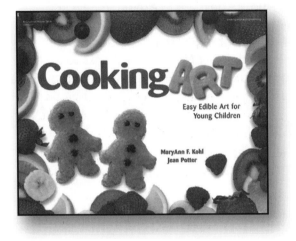

Cooking Art
Easy Edible Art for Young Children
MaryAnn F. Kohl and Jean Potter

Transform the classroom into an artist's studio with these easy edible art experiences. Organized by theme, such as Shapes & Forms and Color & Design, **Cooking Art** combines the familiar area of art exploration with the fascinating world of cooking, including all of its wondrous tools, tastes, and outcomes. Includes recipes for snacks, sandwiches, drinks, desserts, breads, and fruit, as well as pet treats. Each recipe allows ample room for cooking artists to explore and create in their own special, unique ways. 192 pages. 1997.

"Fun in its simplest, purest, most delightful form…" —*Joyful Child Journal*

ISBN 0-87659-184-5 / Gryphon House / 18237 / PB

Preschool Art
It's the Process, Not the Product
MaryAnn F. Kohl

Anyone working with preschoolers and early primary age children will want this book. Over 200 activities encourage children to explore and understand their world through art experiences that emphasize the process of art, not the product. The first chapter introduces basic art activities appropriate for all children, while the subsequent chapters, which build on the basic activities in the first chapter, are divided by seasons. Activities are included for painting, drawing, collage, sculpture and construction. Indexes organized by art medium and project name help teachers plan. 260 pages. 1994.

"…Preschool Art is an essential addition to preschool, day care center, and kindergarten reference shelves…" —*Wisconsin Bookwatch*

ISBN 0-87659-168-3 / Gryphon House / 16985 / PB

Available at your favorite bookstore, school supply store or order from Gryphon House

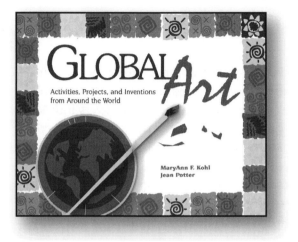

Global Art

Activities, Projects, and Inventions from Around the World

MaryAnn F. Kohl and Jean Potter

An ideal way to start children on an exciting, creative adventure toward global understanding! Over 135 fun, easy-to-do art activities in *Global Art* use collage, painting, drawing, printing, construction, and sculpture to help children appreciate people and cultures from all over the world. Each activity is explained in step-by-step detail and accompanied by geographic and cultural background to help you make the most of the teaching possibilities. Each project is accompanied by a map showing the geographic location of its source and fascinating information on its native land, culture or history. 190 pages. 1998.

"A must-have for teachers and parents who are looking for a lot of ideas, well packaged, in an affordable format." — *Children's Literature*

ISBN 0-87659-190-X / Gryphon House / 18827 / PB

Making Make-Believe

Fun Props, Costumes and Creative Play Ideas

MaryAnn F. Kohl

Explore the world of make-believe with fun and easy-to-make props and costumes. Create a lifesize igloo out of milk jugs or put on a puppet show in your very own Lighted Box Stage! *Making Make-Believe* offers storybook play, games, cooking, mini-plays, dress-up costumes, puppet ideas, and more, to enrich children's play. Unlock the imaginations of young children, allowing them to create their own dramatic play experiences. With over 125 activities and projects, this book is packed with ideas for hours of creative fun! 192 pages. 1999.

ISBN 0-87659-198-5 / Gryphon House / 19674 / PB

Available at your favorite bookstore, school supply store or order from Gryphon House

Recommended Titles

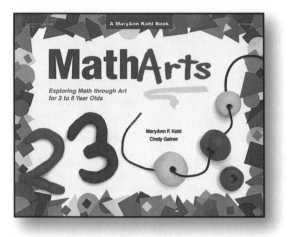

MathArts
Exploring Math Through Art for 3 to 6 Year Olds

MaryAnn F. Kohl and and Cindy Gainer

Get ready to create and count in an exciting introduction to math! This innovative book uses creative art projects to introduce early math concepts. Each of the 200 hands-on projects is designed to help children discover essential math skills through a creative process unique to every individual. This well-organized book provides both teachers and parents with a diverse range of activities for making math both fun and fascinating. The possibilities are endless! 256 pages. 1996.

"Teachers who have the responsibility and pleasure of introducing very young children to mathematics will find many worthwhile activities in *MathArts*. Children, often unknowingly, are surrounded by mathematics in their day to day lives. *MathArts* helps them recognize that fact and become more comfortable using beginning mathematic skills.
—*Teaching Children Mathematics Magazine*

ISBN 0-87659-177-2 / Gryphon House / 16987 / PB

(Almost) Everything You Need to Know About Early Childhood Education
The Book of Lists for Teachers and Parents

Judy Fujawa

Veteran teacher Judy Fujawa offers over two decades of experience in her warm, witty book of lists. From the practical to the philosophic to the hilarious, these lists cover nearly everything one needs to know to work with and raise young children. 128 pages. 1998.

"Whether it's fun things to put in the water table or how to prepare children for kindergarten or things to do with boxes, you can always rely on *(Almost) Everything You Need to Know About Early Childhood Education* for useful, creative, effective ideas." —*Wisconsin Bookwatch*

ISBN 0-87659-192-6 / Gryphon House / 18275 / PB

Available at your favorite bookstore, school supply store or order from Gryphon House

Transition Tips and Tricks For Teachers

Jean Feldman

The author of the best-selling book *Transition Time* brings you more attention-grabbing, creative activities that turn potentially stressful transitions into fun learning experiences. Provide children with an outlet for wiggles, while giving their brains a jump start with cross-lateral movement games. Grab their attention with songs, games, and fingerplays for any time of the day, such as Freddie Flea (who even does tricks—but only if it's very, very quiet). These classroom-tested ideas are sure to become favorites!

ISBN 0-87659-216-7 / Gryphon House / 16728 / PB

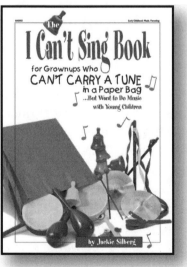

The I Can't Sing Book

For Grownups Who Can't Carry a Tune in a Paper Bag But Want to Do Music with Young Children

Jackie Silberg

Who says you need an opera singer's voice to teach music to young children? Fascinating, easy activities help even the most tone-deaf adult show children the wonder and magic of making and hearing music. All you need are things like rubber bands, paper clips, jingle bells and paper plates to bring the joy of music to children. 174 pages. 1998.

"…This will prove a lifesaver for anyone working with kids who wants to do music with youngsters! Chapters provide some new approaches to musical development for all ages." —*Wisconsin Bookwatch*

ISBN 0-87659-191-8 / Gryphon House / 15921 / PB

Available at your favorite bookstore, school supply store or order from Gryphon House

Recommended Titles

The GIANT Encyclopedia of Art and Craft Activities

Edited by Kathy Charner

Teacher created, classroom-tested art activities to actively engage children's imaginations! The result of a nationwide competition, these art and craft activities are the best of the best. Just the thing to add pizazz to your day!

The GIANT Encyclopedia of Art and Craft Activities joins our best-selling GIANT Encyclopedia series which includes *The GIANT Encyclopedia of Circle Time and Group Activities*, *The GIANT Encyclopedia of Theme Activities*, and *The GIANT Encyclopedia of Science Activities*.

ISBN 0-87659-209-4 / Gryphon House / 16854 / PB

The GIANT Encyclopedia of Science Activities

More Than 600 Science Activities for Children 3 to 6

Edited by Kathy Charner

Leave your fears of science behind as our GIANT Encyclopedia authors have done. Respond to children's natural curiosity with over 600 teacher-created, classroom-tested activities guaranteed to teach your children all about science while they are having fun. The result of a nationwide contest, *The GIANT Encyclopedia of Science Activities* joins our best selling GIANT Encyclopedia series. 575 pages. 1998.

"Teachers of three to six-year olds will not relinquish their copy, so media centers had better have more than one." —*Children's Literature*

ISBN 0-87659-193-4 / Gryphon House / 18325 / PB

Available at your favorite bookstore, school supply store or order from Gryphon House

The Giant Encyclopedia of Theme Activities for Children 2 to 5

Over 600 Favorite Activities

Created by Teachers for Teachers

Edited by Kathy Charner

This popular potpourri of over 600 classroom-tested activities actively engages children's imaginations and provides many months of learning fun. Organized into 48 popular themes, from Dinosaurs to Circus to Outer Space, these favorites are the result of a nationwide competition. 511 pages. 1993.

"What a fantastic idea!…We've added this super compendium to our staff resource room–it's a must!" —*Early Childhood News*

ISBN 0-87659-166-7 / Gryphon House / 19216 / PB

The Giant Encyclopedia of Circle Time and Group Activities for Children 3 to 6

Over 600 Favorite Activities Created by Teachers for Teachers

Edited by Kathy Charner

Open to any page in this book and you will find an activity for circle or group time written by an experienced teacher. Filled with over 600 activities covering 48 themes, this book is jam-packed with ideas that were tested by teachers in the classroom. 510 pages. 1996.

"…open this book anywhere and find something fun to do…teachers with years of experience should find great new suggestions here, while beginners will find it invaluable."—*Notes from The Window Sill*

ISBN 0-87659-181-0 / Gryphon House / 16413 / PB

Recommended Titles

Never, EVER, Serve Sugary Snacks on Rainy Days

The Official Little Instruction

Book for Teachers of Young Children

Shirley Raines
Filled with warm and witty words of wisdom—the perfect gift for teachers of young children. It's light, it's funny, and it goes straight to the heart. 192 pages. 1995.

ISBN 0-87659-175-6 / Gryphon House / 18645 / PB

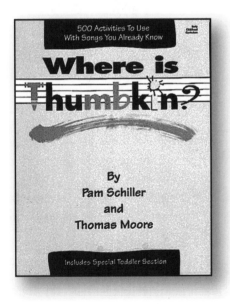

Where Is Thumbkin?

500 Activities to Use with Songs You Already Know

Pam Schiller and Thomas Moore
Sing over 200 familiar songs and learn new words set to familiar tunes. Organized by month, with a special section just for toddlers, this book provides easy song-related activities that span the curriculum in areas such as math, art and language. A finalist for the 1994 Ben Franklin Award. 256 pages. 1993.

ISBN 0-87659-164-0 / Gryphon House / 13156 / PB

Available at your favorite bookstore, school supply store or order from Gryphon House

Recommended Titles

Squish, Sort, Paint & Build
Over 200 Easy Learning Center Activities

Sharon MacDonald

Enrich classroom learning centers with lively, fun activities designed to stimulate learning for young children. This essential resource includes over 200 activities for the following centers: Manipulatives, Construction, Woodworking, Blocks, Music, Gross Motor, Library, Science, Dramatic Play, Art, and Sand and Water. 272 pages. 1996.

"…This book is about how to make learning fun and exciting." —*Florida Primary Educator*

ISBN 0-87659-180-2 / Gryphon House 16395 / PB

The Complete Resource Book
An Early Childhood Curriculum
Over 2000 Activities and Ideas

Pam Schiller and Kay Hastings

The Complete Resource Book is an absolute must-have book for every teacher. Offering a complete plan for every day of every week of the year, this is an excellent reference book for responding to children's specific interests.

Each daily plan contains:
- circle time activities
- music and movement activities
- suggested books
- six learning center ideas

The appendix, jam-packed with songs, recipes, and games, is almost a book in itself. **The Complete Resource Book** is like a master teacher working at your side, offering you guidance and inspiration all year long. 463 pages. 1998.

ISBN 0-87659-195-0 / Gryphon House / 15327 / PB

Available at your favorite bookstore, school supply store or order from Gryphon House